First World War
and Army of Occupation
War Diary
France, Belgium and Germany

23 DIVISION
69 Infantry Brigade,
Brigade Machine Gun Company
19 February 1916 - 1 November 1917

WO95/2184/5

The Naval & Military Press Ltd
www.nmarchive.com
Published in association with The National Archives

Published by

The Naval & Military Press Ltd

Unit 10 Ridgewood Industrial Park,
Uckfield, East Sussex,
TN22 5QE England
Tel: +44 (0) 1825 749494

www.naval-military-press.com
www.nmarchive.com

This diary has been reprinted in facsimile from the original. Any imperfections are inevitably reproduced and the quality may fall short of modern type and cartographic standards.

© Crown Copyright
Images reproduced by permission of The National Archives, London, England, 2015.

Contents

Document type	Place/Title	Date From	Date To
Heading	WO95/2184/5 Brigade Machine Gun Company		
Heading	23rd Division 69th Infy Bde 69th Machine Gun Coy. Feb 1916-1917 Oct To Italy.		
Heading	69th Bde M.G.Coy Vol 1 23 Div 23 Feb16 Dec18		
War Diary	Grantham	19/02/1916	23/02/1916
War Diary	Southampton	24/02/1916	24/02/1916
War Diary	Southampton Water	25/02/1916	26/02/1916
War Diary	Southampton	27/02/1916	01/03/1916
War Diary	Le Havre	02/03/1916	02/03/1916
War Diary	Bleville	03/03/1916	03/03/1916
War Diary	Maisnil-Le-Ruitz	03/03/1916	04/03/1916
War Diary	Grande Servins	05/03/1916	05/03/1916
War Diary	Souchez	07/03/1916	10/03/1916
War Diary	Gouy Servins	11/03/1916	12/03/1916
War Diary	Bruay	13/03/1916	18/03/1916
War Diary	Hersin	19/03/1916	19/03/1916
War Diary	P & Sains	20/03/1916	31/03/1916
War Diary	P & Sains (fosse 10)	01/04/1916	01/04/1916
War Diary	P & Sains	02/04/1916	16/04/1916
War Diary	Hersin.	17/04/1916	17/04/1916
War Diary	Beugin.	18/04/1916	18/04/1916
War Diary	Fiefs	19/04/1916	19/04/1916
War Diary	Vincly	20/04/1916	25/04/1916
War Diary	Hersin	26/04/1916	01/05/1916
Heading	Co 69 Machine Gun Company Operation Order. Appendix A.		
Miscellaneous			
Miscellaneous	D.A.G. 3rd Echelon	03/06/1916	03/06/1916
War Diary	Hersin	01/05/1916	05/05/1916
War Diary	Beugin	06/05/1916	10/05/1916
War Diary	Hersin	11/05/1916	11/05/1916
War Diary	P & Sains.	12/05/1916	29/05/1916
War Diary	Bouvigny	30/05/1916	08/06/1916
War Diary	Aix Noulette	09/06/1916	11/06/1916
War Diary	Boyeffles	12/06/1916	13/06/1916
War Diary	Calonne Ricouart	14/06/1916	15/06/1916
War Diary	Liettres	16/06/1916	24/06/1916
War Diary	Bertangles	25/06/1916	30/06/1916
War Diary	Coisy Baizieux	01/07/1916	01/07/1916
War Diary	Baizieux	01/07/1916	01/07/1916
War Diary	Albert	02/07/1916	02/07/1916
War Diary	Becourt Wood	03/07/1916	05/07/1916
War Diary	Trenches Scots Rdt.	06/07/1916	06/07/1916
War Diary	Albert	07/07/1916	07/07/1916
War Diary	Trenches And Albert	08/07/1916	08/07/1916
War Diary	Becourt Wood And Trenches.	10/07/1916	11/07/1916
War Diary	Albert	12/07/1916	12/07/1916
War Diary	Franvillers	13/07/1916	13/07/1916
War Diary	Molliens Aux Bois	14/07/1916	14/07/1916
War Diary	Molliens Sec	15/07/1916	17/07/1916

War Diary	Molliens	18/07/1916	20/07/1916
War Diary	Millencourt	21/07/1916	25/07/1916
War Diary	Albert	26/07/1916	27/07/1916
War Diary	Trenches Martinpuich	28/07/1916	31/07/1916
War Diary	Albert	01/08/1916	01/08/1916
Miscellaneous	Report On Operations Carried Out From 3rd To The 6th Appendix A.	07/07/1916	07/07/1916
Miscellaneous	Report On Operations Carried Out At Contalmaison On The 10th-11th July 1916. Appendix B.		
Heading	69th Brigade 23rd Division 69th Brigade Machine Gun Company August 1916		
War Diary	Albert	01/08/1916	04/08/1916
War Diary	Trenches SW Martin Puich	05/08/1916	05/08/1916
War Diary	Trenches S.W. Martin Puich	06/08/1916	06/08/1916
War Diary	Trenches And Bresle	07/08/1916	07/08/1916
War Diary	Bresle	08/08/1916	10/08/1916
War Diary	Vauchelles	11/08/1916	13/08/1916
War Diary	Bailleul	13/08/1916	13/08/1916
War Diary	R31 X1	14/08/1916	14/08/1916
War Diary	Trois Arbres	15/08/1916	15/08/1916
War Diary	Ploegsteert	16/08/1916	01/09/1916
Miscellaneous	No by Coy & Gun Corps Appendix 'A'	31/08/1916	31/08/1916
War Diary	Ploegsteert	01/09/1916	04/09/1916
War Diary	S27B.	05/09/1916	05/09/1916
War Diary	Bailleul	06/09/1916	06/09/1916
War Diary	Stomer	06/09/1916	06/09/1916
War Diary	Petit Difques	06/09/1916	10/09/1916
War Diary	Longueau	11/09/1916	11/09/1916
War Diary	Poulainville	11/09/1916	12/09/1916
War Diary	Henencourt Wood	12/09/1916	15/09/1916
War Diary	Millencourt	16/09/1916	17/09/1916
War Diary	Martinpuich	18/09/1916	22/09/1916
War Diary	Lonely Trench	22/09/1916	25/09/1916
War Diary	Contalmaison	26/09/1916	01/10/1916
Miscellaneous	To Staff Captain. 69th Infantry Brigade Attached herewith Please Find War Diary In Duplicate For The Month Of October 1916	03/11/1916	03/11/1916
War Diary	Contalmaison	01/10/1916	01/10/1916
War Diary	Le Sars	02/10/1916	08/10/1916
War Diary	Lonely Trench Albert	09/10/1916	09/10/1916
War Diary	Albert	10/10/1916	12/10/1916
War Diary	Yvrencheux.	13/10/1916	13/10/1916
War Diary	Yvrencheux	14/10/1916	14/10/1916
War Diary	Poperinghe	15/10/1916	22/10/1916
War Diary	Zillebeke	23/10/1916	01/11/1916
Miscellaneous	69th M.G.C. Appendix.		
War Diary	Zillebeke.	01/11/1916	03/11/1916
War Diary	Erie Camp	04/11/1916	09/11/1916
War Diary	Zillebeke	09/11/1916	21/11/1916
War Diary	Erie Camp	22/11/1916	28/11/1916
War Diary	Zillebeke	29/11/1916	14/12/1916
War Diary	Erie Camp	15/12/1916	21/12/1916
War Diary	Erie Camp Zillebeke.	22/12/1916	22/12/1916
War Diary	Zillebeke.	23/12/1916	06/01/1917
War Diary	Zillebeke Eric Camp.	07/01/1917	14/01/1917
War Diary	Ypres.	15/01/1917	31/01/1917

War Diary	Erie Camp	01/02/1917	07/02/1917
War Diary	Erie Camp Zillebeke.	08/02/1917	08/02/1917
War Diary	Zillebeke	08/02/1917	25/02/1917
War Diary	Erie Camp	26/02/1917	27/02/1917
War Diary	Herzeele	27/02/1917	28/02/1917
War Diary	Merckeghem Bayenghem Les-Eperleques.	01/03/1917	01/03/1917
War Diary	Bayenghem	02/03/1917	18/03/1917
War Diary	Bayenghem Merkeghem.	19/03/1917	19/03/1917
War Diary	Merkeghem Houtkerque	20/03/1917	20/03/1917
War Diary	Houtkerque "Y" Camp	21/03/1917	21/03/1917
War Diary	Y Camp	22/03/1917	01/04/1917
Miscellaneous	To. Staff Captain 69th. Infantry Brigade.	11/04/1917	11/04/1917
War Diary	Y Camp	01/04/1917	05/04/1917
War Diary	Y Camp Toronto	06/04/1917	06/04/1917
War Diary	Toronto Camp	07/04/1917	11/04/1917
War Diary	Toronto Winnipeg Camp	12/04/1917	12/04/1917
War Diary	Winnipeg Camp	13/04/1917	14/04/1917
War Diary	Winnipeg Camp Hill Co	15/04/1917	15/04/1917
War Diary	Hill 60	22/04/1917	26/04/1917
War Diary	Steenvoorde	01/05/1917	10/05/1917
War Diary	Winnipeg Camp	10/05/1917	18/05/1917
War Diary	Hill 60	18/05/1917	24/05/1917
War Diary	Boeschepe	24/05/1917	02/06/1917
War Diary	Boeschepe Ouderdom	03/06/1917	03/06/1917
War Diary	Ouderdom	04/06/1917	05/06/1917
War Diary	Hill 60	05/06/1917	11/06/1917
War Diary	Hill 60 Vancouver Camp	12/06/1917	12/06/1917
War Diary	Vancouver Camp	13/06/1917	13/06/1917
War Diary	Roukloshille	13/06/1917	28/06/1917
War Diary	Zevecoten	29/06/1917	29/06/1917
War Diary	In The Line	29/06/1917	30/06/1917
Operation(al) Order(s)	Operation Order No 10 By Captain M. Freeman Commanding 69th Company Machine Gun Corps. Appendix "A".	03/06/1917	03/06/1917
Miscellaneous	69th Company Machine Gun Corps. Appendix "B".	07/06/1917	07/06/1917
Miscellaneous	69th Company Machine Gun Corps. Appendix C.		
War Diary	Bluff	01/07/1917	04/07/1917
War Diary	Steenvoorde	05/07/1917	11/07/1917
War Diary	Steenvoorde Micmac Camp.	12/07/1917	12/07/1917
War Diary	Micmac Camp.	13/07/1917	13/07/1917
War Diary	H 31 Control (Sheet 28).	13/07/1917	13/07/1917
War Diary	Micmac Camp.	13/07/1917	14/07/1917
War Diary	Micmac Camp Hill 60	14/07/1917	14/07/1917
War Diary	Hill 60	15/07/1917	22/07/1917
War Diary	Micmac Camp	23/07/1917	23/07/1917
War Diary	Meteren	24/07/1917	25/07/1917
War Diary	Meteren Petit Difques	26/07/1917	26/07/1917
War Diary	Petit Difques	27/07/1917	08/08/1917
War Diary	Petit Difques Le Bas de Moulle	09/08/1917	09/08/1917
War Diary	Le Bas De Moulle	10/08/1917	23/08/1917
War Diary	Near Abeele.	24/08/1917	25/08/1917
War Diary	Dickebusch	26/08/1917	01/09/1917
Miscellaneous	To Staff Captain 69 Inf Brigade	04/10/1917	04/10/1917
War Diary	Dickebusch	01/09/1917	01/09/1917
War Diary	Steenvoorde	02/09/1917	02/09/1917
War Diary	Lederzeele	03/09/1917	13/09/1917

War Diary	Steenvoorde	14/09/1917	14/09/1917
War Diary	Ontario Camp Reninghelst	15/09/1917	15/09/1917
War Diary	Micmac Camp	16/09/1917	19/09/1917
War Diary	Stirling Castle	20/09/1917	24/09/1917
War Diary	Ontario Camp	25/09/1917	01/10/1917
Operation(al) Order(s)	Operation Order No 26 Appendix A	17/09/1917	17/09/1917
Operation(al) Order(s)	Administrative Arrangements In Connection with Operation Order No. 26 by Capt. M. Freeman M.C., Commanding 69th Company Machine Gun Corps. Appendix B.	18/09/1917	18/09/1917
Miscellaneous	No. 69 Coy. In. Gun Corps Appendix "C"	19/09/1917	19/09/1917
Operation(al) Order(s)	Operation Order No 27. Appendix "D"	23/09/1917	23/09/1917
Miscellaneous	No 69 Coy & Bn Corps. Detailed List of Casualties From 27.9.17 To 2.10.17. Appendix "E".	27/09/1917	27/09/1917
Miscellaneous	Action Of 69th Company Machine Gun Corps From the night 19th /20th to 23rd September 1917. Appendix "F".	19/09/1917	19/09/1917
Miscellaneous	23rd Div. S.G.181/1/2	26/09/1917	26/09/1917
Miscellaneous	A Form. Messages And Signals.		
Miscellaneous	O.C. 69th Machine Gun Company	26/09/1917	26/09/1917
Miscellaneous	The Following Statements were made by Prisoners as to the effect of our M.G. Barrage on September 20th:-	25/09/1917	25/09/1917
Miscellaneous	O.C. 69th Machine Gun Company.	26/09/1917	26/09/1917
War Diary	O.G. 69 M.G. Coy.	03/10/1917	03/10/1917
Miscellaneous		03/10/1917	03/10/1917
War Diary	Clapham Junction	02/10/1917	02/10/1917
War Diary	Ridgewood	03/10/1917	03/10/1917
War Diary	Meteren	04/10/1917	10/10/1917
War Diary	Ontario Camp	11/09/1917	16/09/1917
War Diary	Mound	17/10/1917	22/10/1917
War Diary	Anzac Camp	23/10/1917	23/10/1917
War Diary	Westbecourt	24/10/1917	01/11/1917

WO 95

2184/5

Brigade Machine gun Company.

23RD DIVISION
69TH INFY BDE

69TH MACHINE GUN COY.

FEB 1916 - ~~DEC 1918~~ 1917 OCT

TO ITALY

Feb '16
Dec '18

69th Bde
M. G. Coy
Vol 1

23rd Div
23

Instructions regarding War Diaries and Intelligence Summaries are contained in F. S. Regs., Part II. and the Staff Manual respectively. Title pages will be prepared in manuscript.

WAR DIARY

~~or~~

~~INTELLIGENCE SUMMARY.~~

(~~Erase heading not required~~.) No. 69. Machine Gun Company. Feb 19th – 29th 1916

Army Form C. 2118.

Place	Date	Hour	Summary of Events and Information	Remarks and references to Appendices
Grantham	19.II.16	10.p.m	Received orders to proceed Overseas on Monday 21st inst.	W.P.
GRANTHAM	20.II.16	10.p.m	Orders cancelled. Orders to proceed overseas Wednesday 23rd inst.	W.P.
GRANTHAM.	21.II.16	10.p.m	Company paraded and warned.	W.P.
GRANTHAM.	22.II.16	10.p.m	Detailed orders received as to entrainment etc.	W.P.
GRANTHAM	23.II.16	10.p.m	Company marches off to entrain at Grantham Station at 11.40.p.m.	W.P.
SOUTHAMPTON	24.II.16	10.p.m	Company entrained at 4.0.A.M and detrained at SOUTHAMPTON at 2.0.p.m. Embarked forthwith on H.M Troopship AUSTRALIND. The Ship sailed at 5.0.p.m and dropped anchor at 5.30.p.m in SOUTHAMPTON WATER.	W.P.
SOUTHAMPTON WATER.	25.II.16	10.p.m	Weighed anchor and sailed at about 5.p.m. after reaching boom at NO MAN'S FORT, turned back and dropped anchor at original position	W.P.
SOUTHAMPTON WATER.	26.II.16	10.p.m	No Change.	W.P.
SOUTHAMPTON	27.II.16	10.p.m	No change.	W.P.
" "	28.II.16	10.p.m	No change.	W.P.
" "	29.II.16	10.p.m	Weighed Anchor and sailed. After proceeding a few miles escort gave orders for us to return immediately owing to danger from enemy submarines	W.P.

T2134. Wt. W708–776. 500000. 4/15. Sir J. C. & S.

Instructions regarding War Diaries and Intelligence Summaries are contained in F. S. Regs., Part II. and the Staff Manual respectively. Title pages will be prepared in manuscript.

WAR DIARY
~~or~~
~~INTELLIGENCE SUMMARY.~~
(~~Erase heading not required.~~)

Army Form C. 2118.

NO 69. MACHINE GUN COMPANY. March 1st – 31st.

Place	Date	Hour	Summary of Events and Information	Remarks and references to Appendices
SOUTHAMPTON	1. III. 16.	10 p.m.	Weighed anchor and sailed at 5 p.m. accompanied by escort of 2 Destroyers.	[initials]
LE HAVRE	2. III. 16.	10 p.m.	Arrived LE HAVRE at 9.0 A.M. Company disembarked. Met officer i/c advance party drew remainder of Mobilization stores. Received orders to march to rest camp at BLEVILLE.	[initials]
BLEVILLE.	3. III. 16	1.0 a.m.	Received orders to entrain at Point 6. LE HAVRE at 3.30 p.m.	[initials]
MAISNIL-LE-RUITZ	3. III. 16.	10 p.m.	Detrained at BRUAY at about 12 noon reported arrival by wire to 69th INF. BGDE. to which formation the company is attached. Recd orders from 69th Brigade to march to billets at MAISNIL-LE-RUITZ. Reported personally to Brigade H^d Qrs at RUITZ. Received orders for 2 sections to be attached to 9th Yorkshire regiment and to march with them tomorrow morning.	[initials]
MAISNIL-LE-RUITZ	4. III. 16.	10 p.m.	Two sections marched off with 9th Yorkshire Regt at 11.0 A.M. to billets in ~~[illegible]~~ GOUY SERVINS. Received orders for remainder of company to march with the Brigade tomorrow morning.	[initials]
GRANDE SERVINS.	5. III. 16.	10 p.m.	Company less 2 sections with 9th Yorks arrived in billets here at 5 p.m.	[initials]
SOUCHEZ.	7. III. 16.	10 p.m.	The whole company is now in the SOUCHEZ Sector. The company relieved the	[initials]

T2134. Wt. W708—776. 500000. 4/15. Sir J. C. & S.

WAR DIARY
or
INTELLIGENCE SUMMARY.
(Erase heading not required.)

Army Form C. 2118.

Instructions regarding War Diaries and Intelligence Summaries are contained in F. S. Regs., Part II. and the Staff Manual respectively. Title pages will be prepared in manuscript.

No 69. MACHINE GUN COMPANY.

Place	Date	Hour	Summary of Events and Information	Remarks and references to Appendices
(Continued.)				
SOUCHEZ.	7.III.16	—	french troops when the Brigade took over the SOUCHEZ SECTOR, owing to the smallness of present Establishment of M.G. Companies the men had to suffer unnecessary hardships in carrying Guns ammunition etc. through communication trenches 4 or 5 Kilometres long in a heavy snowstorm. Trenches extremely bad and mud several feet deep in most places. The French troops leave their trenches in a filthy condition.	[illegible]
SOUCHEZ	8.III.16	10 p.m.	Enemy artillery fairly active at noon today otherwise no change.	[illegible]
SOUCHEZ	9.III.16	10 p.m.	No change.	[illegible]
SOUCHEZ	10.III.16	10 p.m.	Company is being relieved tonight by No 24. M.G. Coy as the Brigade is being relieved by the 24th Brigade. Guns and ammunition are left in the trenches in accordance with Div. orders.	[illegible]
GOUY SERVINS	11.III.16	10 p.m.	The company arrived to Billets here early this morning, with the exception of one section (4 guns) which has to go into reserve trenches at NOTRE DAME DE LORETTE Spur with 9th Yorkshire Regiment. One casualty occurred while in the trenches of an accidental nature. Applied to Brigade for some infantry men to be attached for duty to Coy to make up for smallness of Establishment.	[illegible]
GOUY SERVINS	12.III.16	10 p.m.	Received orders to march with Brigade to billets in BRUAY tomorrow morning at 12 hrs.	[illegible]
BRUAY	13.III.16	10 p.m.	The Company marched off from GOUY SERVINS in accordance with fresh orders from Brigade at 10 A.M. arrived BRUAY about 3.30 p.m.	[illegible]

T2134. Wt. W708—776. 500000. 4/15. Sir J. C. & S.

Instructions regarding War Diaries and Intelligence Summaries are contained in F. S. Regs., Part II. and the Staff Manual respectively. Title pages will be prepared in manuscript.

WAR DIARY
or
INTELLIGENCE SUMMARY.
(Erase heading not required.)

Army Form C. 2118.

No 69. M.G. Coy.

Place	Date	Hour	Summary of Events and Information	Remarks and references to Appendices
BRUAY	14.III.16	10 p.m.	Sixteen men admitted to Hospital mostly suffering from trench feet. otherwise no change.	LWP
BRUAY	15.III.16	10 p.m.	no change.	
BRUAY	16.III.16	10 p.m.	The Company was inspected by the Brigadier General assisted by O.C. 24 M.G. Coy. The General expressed his satisfaction at the standard of efficiency reached during the short time the coy has been formed.	LWP
BRUAY	17.III.16	10 p.m.	no change.	LWP
BRUAY	18.III.16	[illegible] p.m.	Received orders to move to HERSIN today preparatory to relieving the 5th Brigade 2nd Division in the ANGRES Sector.	LWP
HERSIN	19.III.16	10 A.M.	Company arrived to Billets here this evening at about 5. p.m.	LWP
Pt SAINS	20.III.16	10 p.m.	Company marched off from HERSIN yesterday morning at 6.30 A.M. and marched by circuitous routes to BULLY-GRENAY from whence the transport returned to Pt SAINS where Coy Hd Qrs are situated, FOSSE.10. the coy relieved no 5 M.G. Coy in the ANGRES sector. Short but fairly heavy bombardment of centre Battalion in trenches at about 7.30 p.m. 2 Zeppelins reported close to here.	LWP

T2134. Wt. W708—776. 500000. 4/15. Sir J. C. & S.

Instructions regarding War Diaries and Intelligence Summaries are contained in F. S. Regs., Part II. and the Staff Manual respectively. Title pages will be prepared in manuscript.

WAR DIARY
or
~~INTELLIGENCE~~ SUMMARY.

(~~Erase heading not required.~~)

Army Form C. 2118.

No. 69. M. G. Coy

Place	Date	Hour	Summary of Events and Information	Remarks and references to Appendices
Pt SAINS.	21.III.16.	10 p.m.	~~2/Lieut C.W.F. Woolnough~~ 2/Lt. C.W.F. WOOLNOUGH of this coy was killed by a piece of Shrapnel shell which struck him on the head at 10. p.m today. He was buried by C of E Chaplain at 7.30.p.m. Otherwise no change	WAP
Pt SAINS.	22.III.16	10 p.m.	No change. Rain. one Gun team relieved (1 N.C.O. 5 men)	WAP
Pt SAINS.	23.III.16	10 p.m.	2/Lt DE VILLIERS appointed town Major for FOSSE. 10. 1 gun team relieved	WAP
Pt SAINS.	24.III.16	10 p.m.	No change. Heavy snowstorm. 1 gun team relieved	WAP
Pt SAINS.	25.III.16	10 p.m.	Owing to melting snow trenches have become very bad. 1 gun team relieved	WAP
Pt SAINS.	26.III.16	10 p.m.	There are altogether 10 guns in the trenches and 6 in billets at FOSSE 10. as some men (16) are in hospital it is impossible to relieve the men in the trenches more often than once every 10 days. By relieving 1 gun team (1 N.C.O and 5 men) every day, each man is 4 days in billets and 10 days in trenches. In response to my request of 11.III.16 I received 6 men from each Regiment in the Brigade (total 24) to be permanently attached to this company to assist in making up the shortage in the establishment of the company. (one gun team relieved)	WAP

T2134. Wt. W708—776. 500000. 4/15. Sir J. C. & S.

Instructions regarding War Diaries and Intelligence Summaries are contained in F. S. Regs., Part II. and the Staff Manual respectively. Title pages will be prepared in manuscript.

WAR DIARY

or

~~INTELLIGENCE SUMMARY.~~

(Erase heading not required.)

No. 69. Machine Gun Coy.

Army Form C. 2118.

Place	Date	Hour	Summary of Events and Information	Remarks and references to Appendices
Pt SAINS	27.III.16	10 p.m.	No change. One gun team relieved.	[illegible]
Pt SAINS	28.III.16	10 p.m.	No change. One gun team relieved.	[illegible]
Pt SAINS	29.III.16	10 p.m.	G.O.C. inspected Company billets and Transport lines, he expressed his satisfaction at the condition of same. Owing to the small number of Transport drivers allowed for in Establishment (i.e. 22 men for 53 animals) and owing to several cases of sickness, it was necessary to appeal to the G.O.C. for help in this respect. One gun team relieved.	[illegible]
Pt SAINS	30.III.16	10 p.m.	12 men to assist with Transport were attached to the company by order of the Brigadier from Regiments. One gun team relieved.	[illegible]
Pt SAINS.	31.III.16	10 p.m.	One man killed in Front line. 40. 11 inch Howitzer shells dropped in the Colliery near our Transport lines doing no damage outside the colliery. Owing to fine weather enemy Artillery very active. French Aeroplane brought down in our lines in the afternoon with men killed.	

[illegible] Capt.

Comdg. 69. M.G. Coy. 1.III.16.

T2134. Wt. W708—776. 500000. 4/15. Sir J. C. & S.

Instructions regarding War Diaries and Intelligence Summaries are contained in F. S. Regs., Part II. and the Staff Manual respectively. Title pages will be prepared in manuscript.

WAR DIARY
or
~~INTELLIGENCE SUMMARY.~~
(~~Erase heading not required.~~)

XXIM

69 M.G. Coy
Vol. 3

Army Form C. 2118.

No. 69. M.G. Coy. ~~April~~ 1st – 30th

Place	Date	Hour	Summary of Events and Information	Remarks and references to Appendices
Pt SAINS (FOSSE 10)	1.IV.16	10 p.m.	No change. One gun team relieved.	W.S.
Pt SAINS	2.IV.16	10 p.m.	Machine guns have been firing every night into CITÉ de CAUMENT and in and about LIÉVIN also into ANGRES and enemy trench material dump opposite ANGRES I. Working parties have also been fired on nearly every night. One gun team relieved	W.S.
Pt SAINS.	3.IV.16	10 p.m.	No change. One gun team relieved.	W.S.
Pt SAINS	4.IV.16	10 p.m.	2/Lt HINSELWOOD arrived from Grantham to replace the Officer that was Killed on the 21st of March.	W.S.
Pt SAINS	5.IV.16	10 p.m.	The right gun in front line ANGRES I fired on German working party causing it to disperse it is reported that 10 of the enemy were Killed. One Officer 2/Lt Hinselwood admitted to No 23. C.C.S. sick.	W.S.
Pt SAINS	6.IV.16	10 p.m.	The positions of guns in ANGRES sector have been changed as they now stand there are 4 guns in the front line and 6 in the support line the remaining 6 guns are at Coy HdQrs FOSSE 10. The enemy shell the colliery near our transport lines every evening between 3 p.m and 6 p.m. today they dropped two shells into one of our billets wounding	W.S.

T2134. Wt. W708–776. 500000. 4/15. Sir J. C. & S.

Instructions regarding War Diaries and Intelligence Summaries are contained in F. S. Regs., Part II. and the Staff Manual respectively. Title pages will be prepared in manuscript.

WAR DIARY

~~or~~

~~INTELLIGENCE SUMMARY.~~

(~~Erase heading not required.~~)

Army Form C. 2118.

Place	Date	Hour	Summary of Events and Information	Remarks and references to Appendices
P^t SAINS	6.IV.16. (contd)	10 pm	one old woman seriously and one small child slightly. Reinforcement of 13 men arrived.	[illegible]
P^t SAINS	7.IV.16	10 pm	Received operation order no 44 dated 5th inst and issued my operation order no I accordingly. 9.2 gun in position in support line shelled and ruined a sergt in charge slightly wounded. The gun was not damaged	[illegible] Appendix 'A'
P^t SAINS	8.IV.16	10 pm	Inspected positions prepared for firing in accordance with above mentioned order. no change.	[illegible]
P^t SAINS	9.IV.16	10 pm	Received orders that the operation referred to in Appendix 'A' would take place today. order cancelled at 1.0 p m.	[illegible]
P^t SAINS	10.IV.16	10 pm	Received orders that the operation referred to would take place today. operations commenced punctually and the weather was most favourable. The programme was carried out as ordered with the exception that the intense bombardment lasted 6 minutes instead of one minute. The machine guns fired about 1000 rds each. The enemy retaliated on the 68th Bgde Front and slightly on the 69th Bgde Front there were no casualties in the coy.	[illegible]
P^t SAINS	11.IV.16	10 pm	2/Lt TOYNBEE admitted to hospital with Scarlet Fever. this is a very severe loss to the coy.	[illegible]

T2134. Wt. W708—776. 500000. 4/15. Sir J. C. & S.

Instructions regarding War Diaries and Intelligence Summaries are contained in F. S. Regs., Part II. and the Staff Manual respectively. Title pages will be prepared in manuscript.

WAR DIARY

~~or~~

~~INTELLIGENCE SUMMARY.~~

(~~Erase heading not required.~~)

Army Form C. 2118.

No. 69. M.G. Coy.

Place	Date	Hour	Summary of Events and Information	Remarks and references to Appendices
Pt SAINS.	12.IV.16	10 p.m.	Very quiet day.	W.R.P
Pt SAINS.	13.IV.16	10 p.m.	Received orders with proposed programme of Moves to take place on the brigade being relieved on the 16th inst.	W.R.P
Pt SAINS	14.IV.16	10 p.m.	G.O.C inspected the reinforcement of 13 men which arrived on the 6th inst at my request. These men are nearly all under age and untrained also physically unfit to be machine-gunners. I requested the G.O.C to forward a complaint on the subject.	W.R.P
Pt SAINS	15.IV.16	10 p.m.	Major General Babington comdg the 23rd Division inspected the reinforcement referred to and expressed his opinion that these men were not fitted to be infantry men much less to be machine gunners. FOSSE 10. Shelled intermittently with heavy calibre shells from 8 A.M.	W.R.P
Pt SAINS	16.IV.16.	10 p.m.	Coy relieved in the trenches by 5th Coy. M.G. Corps. relief commenced from BULLY-GRENAY Church at 10. A.M. and completed at 1.0. p.m. Marched to HERSIN leaving FOSSE 10 at 3.30. p.m. arriving in billets at 5.15. p.m.	W.R.P

Instructions regarding War Diaries and Intelligence Summaries are contained in F. S. Regs., Part II. and the Staff Manual respectively. Title pages will be prepared in manuscript.

WAR DIARY
or
~~INTELLIGENCE SUMMARY.~~
(*Erase heading not required.*)

Army Form C. 2118.

69th Coy. M. G. Corps.

Place	Date	Hour	Summary of Events and Information	Remarks and references to Appendices
HERSIN	17.IV	10 pm	Marched from HERSIN to BEUGIN where we took our billets.	W.H.G.
BEUGIN	18.IV	10 pm	Remained at BEUGIN refitting clothing etc.	W.H.G.
FIEFS.	19.IV	10 pm	Marched from BEUGIN to FIEFS leaving at 7.0 A.M and joined the Brigade outside PERNES and marched in Brigade to FIEFS where we dismissed to billets at 1.30 p.m. remainder of Brigade went on to manoeuvre area. One officer admitted to Hospital (2/Lt. R.H. ROHDE.)	W.H.G.
VINCLY	20.IV	10 pm	Marched from FIEFS to VINCLY which is our permanent stopping place for the manoeuvre period. Carried out some manoeuvres under Coy arrangements during the afternoon.	W.H.G.
VINCLY	21.IV.	10 pm	Carried out Brigade manoeuvre lasting from 10 A.M. to 5 p.m. weather good.	W.H.G.
VINCLY	22.IV	10 pm	Carried out company manoeuvres lasting from 9 A.M. to 8 p.m.	W.H.G.
VINCLY	23.IV.	10 p.m.	Company manoeuvres	W.H.G.

T2134. Wt. W708—776. 500000. 4/15. Sir J. C. & S.

Instructions regarding War Diaries and Intelligence Summaries are contained in F. S. Regs., Part II. and the Staff Manual respectively. Title pages will be prepared in manuscript.

WAR DIARY

~~or~~

~~INTELLIGENCE SUMMARY.~~

(~~Erase heading not required~~.)

Army Form C. 2118.

69th Coy. M. G. Corps.

Place	Date	Hour	Summary of Events and Information	Remarks and references to Appendices
VINCLY	24.IV.	10 pm.	Company manoeuvres.	W.H.P.
VINCLY	25.IV.	10 pm.	Company manoeuvres in morning. In the afternoon coy marched to billets in PALFART + LIVOSSART preparatory to move on the 26th.	W.H.P.
HERSIN	26.IV.	10 pm.	Marched from Palfart to PERNES entrained at PERNES with 2 other regiments of the Brigade, detrained at BARLIN and marched to our old billets at HERSIN. The Transport marched from PALFART to HERSIN by Road.	W.H.P.
HERSIN.	27.IV.	10 pm	Remained at HERSIN, dispatched 18 men and 1 cpl to the base for further training. Mine shelled heavily all day.	W.H.P.
HERSIN	28.IV.	10 pm	Working parties sent out to dig in the trenches (80 men).	W.H.P.
HERSIN.	29.IV.	10 pm	Remained in billets. 28 men sent to me for training from the Regiments in the brigade.	W.H.P.
HERSIN	30.IV.	10 pm	Remained in Billets.	
HERSIN.	1.V.	10 pm	War diary complete from 1st – 30th April. 1916.	

Walter [illegible]
Capt.
Comdg 69th Coy M. G. Corps.

T2131. Wt. W708—776. 500000. 4/15. Sir J. C. & S.

SECRET. Appendix, A. War. Diary

Copy.

No 69. Machine Gun Company Operation Order.

No 1.

Map. 1/10,000.

(1) An Artillery, Mortar and grenade attack will be made on the 68th Brigade Front at an early date to be notified later. The 69th Brigade will coperate Infantry will not advance but every effort will be made to induce enemy to believe an assault imminent.

No 2. Operations will consist of four phases.

(A) Wire cutting by Artillery on previous day and morning of operations.

(B) Priliminary slow Bombardment for three hours Culminating an intense Bombardment for one minute.

(C) Smoke attack on the 68th Brigade front to simulate gas during which Artillery will "lift" to the second German support line this is intended to induce the Germans to man their parapets and will last five minutes.

(D) Final intense bombardment of German front line

During (B) as much material damage as possible will be done.

(During (d) the object is to kill Germans.

No 3. The priliminary Bombardment will commence three hours before ZERO time and be chiefly on 68th Brigade frontage and points in rear of German line. IV Corps Counter Battery (9.2" How.) will bombard Puits. 16.

No 4. One minute before ZERO the Bombardment will become intense till ZERO time. When three guns of No 69. Machine Gun Company will fire one belt each at the same time, Two Lewis guns per Battalion in front line will fire two Mags. each.

No 5. At ZERO, one Red rocket will be fired from each Company in 68th Brigade Front line. This will be the signal for the 18 pounders and 4.5" How's to "lift" to German support lines for five minute

SECRET.

Appendix A — War Diary Copy.

No 69 Machine Gun Company Operation Order

Map 1/10,000.

(1) An Artillery, Mortar and grenade attack will be made on the 68th Brigade front at an early date to be notified later the 69th Brigade will support. Infantry will not advance but every effort will be made to induce enemy to believe an assault imminent.

Operations will consist of four phases.

(A) Wire cutting by Artillery on previous day and morning of operations.

(B) Preliminary slow Bombardment for three hours culminating in intense Bombardment for one minute.

(C) Smoke attack on the 68th Brigade front to simulate gas during which Artillery will "lift" to the second German support line. This is intended to induce the Germans to man their parapets and will last five minutes.

(D) Final intense bombardment of German front line.

During (B) as much material damage as possible will be done.

During (D) the object is to kill Germans.

The preliminary Bombardment will commence three hours before ZERO time and be chiefly on 68th Brigade frontage and points in rear of German line. The Corps Counter Battery (9.2" How.) will bombard Point 16.

One minute before ZERO the Bombardment will become intense till ZERO time. When three guns of No 69 Machine Gun Company will fire one belt each at the same time two Lewis guns per Battalion in front line will fire two mags. each.

At ZERO, one Red rocket will be fired from each Company in 68th Brigade Front Line. This will be the signal for the 18 pounders and 4.5" How's to "lift" the German support lines for five minutes

No. 5 (Continued) At the same time smoke candles will be lit along 68th Brigade front.

No. 6 At 0.3 (i.e. three minutes after ZERO) three M. Guns of 69. Machine Gun Company and Lewis guns as before will open rapid fire along enemy's parapet for Two minutes only.

No. 7 At 0.5 one green rocket will be fired from each company in 68th Brigade front line, whereupon all 18 pounders and 4.5" Hows will switch back to Germans Front line for one minute

No. 8 Operations will cease at 0.6. when all guns will to normal zones and stand by.

No. 9 During operations sentries will be reduced to one double sentry per platoon who will be kept under protection as far as possible. Machine gun teams when not firing will will remain in deep dug-outs from Three hours before ZERO till one hour after ZERO. except Officers and N.C.O's as are necessarily employed in supervision.

No. 10 The date and hour of ZERO and arrangement for will be notified later.

No. 11 Advanced H. Qs. of 69 Machine Gun Company will be at M.G.O. dug out at junction of Gumboot Trench and Richard trench for the period of these operations.

No. 12 There will be one Officer with each gun whilst it is firing.

No. 13 The position from which guns will fire are marked on attached immediately the firing has finished (i.e. 0.5) the guns should be taken to deep dug-outs.

No. 5 continued

At the same time smoke candles will be lit along 68th Brigade front.

No. 6

At 0.3 (Three minutes after ZERO) three M. Guns of 69 Machine Gun Company and Lewis guns as before will open rapid fire along enemy parapet for two minutes only.

No. 7

At 0.5. one green rocket will be fired from each company in 68th Brigade front line, whereupon all 18 pounders and 4.5" Hows will switch back to Germans front line for one minute.

No. 8

Operations will cease at 0.6. when all guns will to normal fire and stand by.

No. 9

During operations sentries will be reduced to one double sentry per platoon who will be kept under protection as far as possible. Machine gun teams when not firing will will remain in deep dug-outs from three hours before ZERO till one hour after ZERO. except Officers and N.C.O.s as are necessarily employed in supervision.

No. 10

The date and hour of ZERO and arrangements for will be notified later.

No. 11

Advanced H.Q. of 69 Machine Gun Company will be at M.G.O.'s dug out at junction of Gunboat Trench and Richmond Trench for the period of these operations.

No. 12

There will be one Officer with each gun whilst it is firing.

No. 13

The position from which guns will fire are marked on attached immediately the firing has finished (0.2, 0.5) the guns should be taken to deep dug-outs.

D.A.G.

3rd Echelon.

Enclosed please find war diary of 69th Coy. M.G.C. for the month of May.

A.S. Hinshelwood Lt.

Cmdg. 69th Coy. M.G.C.

3rd 6. 1916

Instructions regarding War Diaries and Intelligence Summaries are contained in F. S. Regs., Part II. and the Staff Manual respectively. Title pages will be prepared in manuscript.

WAR DIARY

or ~~INTELLIGENCE SUMMARY.~~

(Erase heading not required.)

XXIII

Army Form C. 2118.

Vol 4

69th Coy. M. G. Corps May, 1916

Place	Date	Hour	Summary of Events and Information	Remarks and references to Appendices
HERSIN	1.V.16	6 p.m.	Working Parties sent to dig in ANGRES Sector.	W.P.
HERSIN	2.V.16	6 p.m.	No change.	W.P.
HERSIN	3.V.16	6 p.m.	Working Parties sent to ANGRES Sector	W.P.
HERSIN	4.V.16	6 p.m.	No Change	W.P.
HERSIN	5.V.16	6 p.m.	Moved to BEUGIN for one weeks rest	W.P.
BEUGIN	6.V.16	6 p.m.	Coy Inspected by G.O.C. 23rd Division who expressed great satisfaction at the progress made in general efficiency and smartness.	W.P.
BEUGIN	7.V.16	6 p.m.	Coy marched through a gas cloud with Helmets on (P.H). The gas was very strong chlorine. There were no casualties.	W.P.
BEUGIN	8.V.16	6 p.m.	One officer sent to 1st Army Signal school for a course	W.P.
BEUGIN	9.V.16	6 p.m.	Coy inspected in the use and adjustment of Respirators by G.O.C. 69th Infantry Brigade.	W.P.
BEUGIN	10.V.16	6 p.m.	No Change.	
HERSIN	11.V.16	6 p.m.	Move to HERSIN preparatory to relieving No 5 Coy M.G.C.	W.P.

Instructions regarding War Diaries and Intelligence Summaries are contained in F. S. Regs., Part II. and the Staff Manual respectively. Title pages will be prepared in manuscript.

WAR DIARY
~~or~~
~~INTELLIGENCE SUMMARY.~~
(~~Erase heading not required.~~)

Army Form C. 2118.

69th Coy. M.G. Corps.

Place	Date	Hour	Summary of Events and Information	Remarks and references to Appendices
Pt SAINS	12.V.	10 p.m.	Coy Relieved no 5. M.G. Coy in the ANGRES Sector, starting at 2 p.m relief complete at 4 p.m. 8 guns in the line 7 in Reserve.	[illegible]
Pt SAINS	13.V.	10 p.m.	There are three guns in the front line trenches, two in the support line, 7 in the 2nd line (BAJOLLE LINE) 4 at FOSSE 10.	[illegible]
Pt SAINS	14.V.	10 p.m.	Mine at FOSSE 10. heavily shelled. 1500 rds fired into ANGRES.	[illegible]
Pt SAINS	15.V.	10 p.m.	Mine at FOSSE 10 heavily Shelled 2000 rds fired into ANGRE and ROLLENCOURT.	[illegible]
Pt SAINS	16.V.	10 p.m.	Enemy very active with Rifle Grenades 24 dropped about no 16 gun position in the front line. 1500 rds fired into R.E. dump at ANGRES.	[illegible]
Pt SAINS	17.V.	10 p.m.	FOSSE 10 Shelled. fired on enemy R.E dumps at ANGRES and ROLLENCOURT.	
Pt SAINS.	18.V.	10 p.m.	Indirect fire carried out from Ligne Maistre on ANGRES and ROLLENCOURT.	
Pt SAINS.	19.V.	10 p.m.	R.E's fired a mine (2 Tons) under salient in enemy line left of BULLY CRATERS at 6.A.M. with great success. 2 machine Guns fired 1000 rds each in and about the crater one minute after the explosion. Artillery fired 3 salvoes. Enemy artillery replied	

T2134. Wt. W708—776. 500000. 4/15. Sir J. C. & S.

Instructions regarding War Diaries and Intelligence Summaries are contained in F. S. Regs., Part II. and the Staff Manual respectively. Title pages will be prepared in manuscript.

WAR DIARY
or
INTELLIGENCE SUMMARY.
(Erase heading not required.)

Army Form C. 2118.

69th Coy. M.G. Corps.

Place	Date	Hour	Summary of Events and Information	Remarks and references to Appendices
			shortly afterwards with 6 Whizz-Bangs. Our 60 lb. Trench mortars then fired 40 rounds. Enemy retaliated with about 40 rds of shrapnel at 6.30 A.M.	[initials]
Pt SAINS	20.V.	10 p.m.	Very quiet day. Machine guns fired 5000 rds into and about the new crater during the night to prevent work being done.	
Pt SAINS	21.V	10 p.m.	Great activity by enemy artillery. Gas alarm was given at 5. p.m. Lacrymatory shells were fired at 6 inch Batteries near FOSSE. 10. Gas became strong at Fosse 10 at about 6. p.m. There was no harm done. Shelling of Bully Grenay AIX NOULETTE and all Batteries in this vicinity continued all night. This was the result of the enemy attack on VIMY ridge. Gas alarm at 11. p.m.	
Pt SAINS	22.V.	10 p.m.	Shelling continued with considerable violence all day and night. Machine Guns fired all night into new enemy Crater.	
Pt SAINS	23.V.	10 p.m.	About 40 rounds of H.E. Shrapnel fired into our billets and the	

T2134. Wt. W708—776. 500000. 4/15. Sir J. C. & S.

Instructions regarding War Diaries and Intelligence Summaries are contained in F. S. Regs., Part II. and the Staff Manual respectively. Title pages will be prepared in manuscript.

WAR DIARY
~~or~~
~~INTELLIGENCE~~ SUMMARY.
(~~Erase heading not required.~~)

Army Form C. 2118.

69th Coy. M.G. Corps.

Place	Date	Hour	Summary of Events and Information	Remarks and references to Appendices
			remainder of FOSSE. 10. Heavy shelling continued as on previous 2 days.	W.P.
Pt SAINS.	24.V.	6 p.m.	Fairly quiet day. Machine Guns fired indirect on enemy Footways during the day with good observation, range about 1900 yards.	W.P.
Pt. SAINS	25.V.	–	Very Quiet and situation unchanged.	A.S.H.
Pt. SAINS.	26.V.		Section relief at 6. A.M. At about 2 A.M. enemy machine gun in THOMSON'S CRATER engaged & silenced by our fire from No. 16 position.	A.S.H.
Pt SAINS	27.V.	10 AM.	Positions on NOTRE DAME DE LORETTE reconnoitred previous to relieving 24th Coy. General activity on our right + left at night and at 10.50 P.M. S.O.S message from left Battalion, right Brigade, 1st Division received. Message cancelled 11.30 P.M.	A.S.H.
Pt. SAINS.	28.V.	8 AM.	Transport moved from Pt SAINS to BOIS DE FROISSART. Our trench mortars fired 30 rounds + in retaliation the enemy heavily whiz-banged left company left battalion. 3–5 P.M. FOSSE 10 heavily shelled. 3.15 P.M. 2 sections relieved by 2 sections 24th Coy. in ANGRES sector. Reserve section at FOSSE 10 relieved 1 section 24th Coy. on NOTRE DAME DE LORETTE, leaving Pt SAINS at 5.45 P.M.	A.S.H.
Pt. SAINS.	29.V.		Limbers removed from Pt SAINS to BOIS DE FROISSART. Pt SAINS shelled from 5 A.M. – 5 P.M.	A.S.H.

A.S. Humphrey Lt.
Comdg 69 Coy M.G.C.

T2134. Wt. W708–776. 500000. 4/15. Sir J. C. & S.

Instructions regarding War Diaries and Intelligence Summaries are contained in F. S. Regs., Part II. and the Staff Manual respectively. Title pages will be prepared in manuscript.

WAR DIARY
or
~~INTELLIGENCE SUMMARY.~~
(Erase heading not required.)

Army Form C. 2118.

69th Coy. M.G.C.

Place	Date	Hour	Summary of Events and Information	Remarks and references to Appendices
			(contd.)	
Pt. SAINS.	29. v.		Section at CAP DE PONT relieved by 1 section 24th Coy. One section at FOSSE 10	A.H.
~~Pt. SAINS.~~	~~30~~		relieved one section 24th Coy. on NOTRE DAME DE LORETTE.	
BOUVIGNY.	30. v.		Two sections and Headquarters left FOSSE 10 at 2.0 P.M. & proceeded to billets in BOUVIGNY	A.H.
BOUVIGNY	31. v.	7 A.M.	Two hostile aeroplanes appeared over BOUVIGNY flying N.E.	A.H.

A.J. Hinchelwood
Lt. Cmdg. 69th Coy. M.G.C.

T2134. Wt W708—776. 500000. 4/15. Sir J. C. & S.

Instructions regarding War Diaries and Intelligence Summaries are contained in F. S. Regs., Part II. and the Staff Manual respectively. Title pages will be prepared in manuscript.

WAR DIARY
or
~~INTELLIGENCE SUMMARY.~~
(Erase heading not required.)

Army Form C. 2118.

23 JUNE

64 MG Coy

Vol 5

Place	Date	Hour	Summary of Events and Information	Remarks and references to Appendices
BOUVIGNY.	1.6.16		Situation normal. Work on dug outs commenced by 24th Coy. continued in conjunction with R.E.	A.S.H.
BOUVIGNY.	2.6.16	10-11.30 A.M.	Gun position No 5 heavily whizz banged owing to the infantry exposing themselves on the hill side above the trench. 4 5.9's fell in front of No 10. dug out — no damage done. New dug out for No. 10 team found just above the position: less exposed & stronger.	A.S.H.
BOUVIGNY.	3.6.16		Company rendez-vous chosen outside BOUVIGNY for use in the event of the village being shelled & a line run from there to top Brigade line. Transport moved to BOIS DE FROSSART. 8.P.M. Section relief and S.O.S. SOUCHEZ II at same time. S.O.S cancelled at 8.45 P.M.	A.S.H.
BOUVIGNY.	4.6.16		Situation normal.	A.S.H.
BOUVIGNY.	5.6.16		8-9 AM and 2.30-3.0. P.M. No 5 gun position again whizz-banged. No casualties and no damage. A fresh emplacement & dug out discovered for No. III. position, defiladed from front & larger field of fire.	A.S.H.
BOUVIGNY.	6.6.16		Situation normal. 10 boxes S.A.A. sent to MAISTRE line guns to complete establishment of 7 boxes per gun.	A.S.H.
BOUVIGNY.	7.6.16		Details for relief arranged with 68 Coy. and inspection of SOUCHEZ trenches carried out. Situation on NOTRE DAME de LORETTE normal.	A.S.H.

T2134. Wt. W708—776. 500000. 4/15. Sir J. C. & S.

Army Form C. 2118.

Instructions regarding War Diaries and Intelligence Summaries are contained in F. S. Regs., Part II. and the Staff Manual respectively. Title pages will be prepared in manuscript.

WAR DIARY
or
~~INTELLIGENCE~~ SUMMARY.
(Erase heading not required.)

Place	Date	Hour	Summary of Events and Information	Remarks and references to Appendices
BOUVIGNY.	8.6.16		Relief of 10 guns 68 Coy by 10 guns 69 Coy in SOUCHEZ Sector completed. Result — 10 guns 69 Coy in SOUCHEZ trenches, 6 in BOUVIGNY. 8 guns 68 Coy on NOTRE DAME and 8 in AIX NOULETTE. At 10. P.M. 1 gun 69 Coy assisted in small raid on German sap and accounted for most of the German party covering the sap. Gun was taken between the trench & the wire — range 40 yds.	[illegible]
AIX NOULETTE	9.6.16		Headquarters & 6 guns moved into billets at AIX NOULETTE. The STRAIGHT, KELLET LINE and BOSCHE WALK trench mortared throughout the day.	[illegible]
AIX NOULETTE	10.6.16		Situation normal. Gun teams in BAJOLLE LINE relieved.	[illegible]
AIX NOULETTE	11.6.16		Situation unchanged, gun teams in BAJOLLE LINE relieved.	[illegible]
BOYEFFLES	12.6.16.		Company relieved in the SOUCHEZ SECTOR and at AIX NOULETTE by the 140th Coy. M.G.C. 47th Division and moved to billets at BOYEFFLES.	[illegible]
BOYEFFLES	13.6.16.		Billets at BOYEFFLES are good but the village crowded.	
CALONNE-RICOUART	14.6.16		Company marched to billets at CALONNE-RICOUART.	[illegible]
CALONNE-RICOUART	15.6.16		Remained in billets which were fairly good.	[illegible]
LIETTRES	16.6.16.		Company marched to billets at LIETTRES (manœuvre area) near AIRE.	[illegible]

T2134. Wt. W708—776. 500000. 4/15. Sir J. C. & S.

Instructions regarding War Diaries and Intelligence Summaries are contained in F. S. Regs., Part II. and the Staff Manual respectively. Title pages will be prepared in manuscript.

WAR DIARY
or
INTELLIGENCE SUMMARY.
(Erase heading not required.)

Army Form C. 2118.

Place	Date	Hour	Summary of Events and Information	Remarks and references to Appendices
LIETTRES	17.6.16		Company was inspected by G.O.C. Machine Gun Corps (Gen. H. de la C. HILL) who expressed his pleasure at the general smartness in appearance and efficiency. The G.O.C. reported that the 69th Coy. M.G.C. was the best in the Division.	WHP
LIETTRES.	18.6.16.		Company manoeuvres carried out.	WHP
LIETTRES.	19.6.16.		The Brigade took part in a Divisional field day. in which the coy did its allotted task quite successfully.	
LIETTRES.	20.6.16.		Company manoeuvres carried out. The manoeuvres as well as experience in the trenches show that it is impossible to bring more than 8 guns into action with the present establishment of gunners (i.e. 80.) The strength of this coy is at present 240. Even this no leaves us 10 men short of what I consider necessary.	WHP
LIETTRES.	21.6.16.		Company manoeuvres carried out. All stores and officers Kit reduced preparatory to moving and having to travel light.	WHP
LIETTRES.	22.6.16.		Company manoeuvres carried out.	WHP
LIETTRES.	23.6.16.		" " "	WHP

T2134. Wt. W708—776. 500000. 4/15. Sir J. C. & S.

Instructions regarding War Diaries and Intelligence Summaries are contained in F. S. Regs., Part II. and the Staff Manual respectively. Title pages will be prepared in manuscript.

WAR DIARY
or
INTELLIGENCE SUMMARY.
(Erase heading not required.)

Army Form C. 2118.

69th Coy. M.G.C.

Place	Date	Hour	Summary of Events and Information	Remarks and references to Appendices
LIETTRES	24.6.16		Head quarters entrained at BERGUETTE station marching off from LIETTRES at 4.10 A.M. the train left at 9.40 A.M. Trains left at 3 hour intervals each train carrying one regiment complete and one section M.G. Coy. detrained at LONGEAU near AMIENS. marched to billets at BERTANGLES.	W.P.
BERTANGLES	25.6.16		All sections have arrived. no 4, being the last, came in at 10.30.A.M.	W.P.
BERTANGLES	26.6.16		Remained in Billets which are good. though water is scarce.	W.P.
BERTANGLES	27.6.16		No change. Orders re move to MOLLIENS au Boix tonight cancelled.	W.P.
BERTANGLES	28.6.16		No change.	W.P.
BERTANGLES	29.6.16		Brigade Route march. about 11. miles. The Division is now attached to the IInd Corps. for Offensive operations.	W.P. W.P.
BERTANGLES COISY.	30.6.16		Marched to COISY in the evening.	W.P.
BAIZIEUX	1st		War Diary completed. up to 30th ult.	

1/VII/16.

[signature] Capt.
Comdg. 69th Coy. M.G.C.

T2134. Wt. W708—776. 500000. 4/15. Sir J. C. & S.

Instructions regarding War Diaries and Intelligence Summaries are contained in F. S. Regs., Part II. and the Staff Manual respectively. Title pages will be prepared in manuscript.

WAR DIARY
or
~~INTELLIGENCE SUMMARY.~~

(~~Erase heading not required.~~)

Army Form C. 2118.

~~23~~ July

69th Coy. M.G.C. Vol. 6

Place	Date	Hour	Summary of Events and Information	Remarks and references to Appendices
BAIZIEUX.	1.VII.16		Marched from COISY to BAISIEUX in the evening and bivouacked in the wood.	W.P.
ALBERT.	II.VII		Marched from BAISIEUX to ALBERT in the evening, and bivouacked in a field about ½ mile N.W. of ALBERT.	W.P.
BECOURT. WOOD	3.VII.		Took no III section into newly captured line at SCOTS REDOUBT remainder of coy bivouacked in BECOURT WOOD.	W.P.
BECOURT WOOD	4.VII.		See appendix "A".	W.P.
BECOURT WOOD	5.VII.		Battle of HORSESHOE LINE which was captured. Lost 2 officers wounded. 16 other ranks killed and wounded. see Appendix A.	Appendix A, W.P.
TRENCHES. SCOTS. Rdt	6.VII		relieved by 58th and 68th Coy in evening. Lost one officer on the road by shell fire also 3 N.C.O.s and 2 men.	W.P.
ALBERT.	7.VII.		marched from Bivouacs to BELLEVUE FARM remained in support all day marching to BECOURT WOOD in the evening.	W.P.
TRENCHES and ALBERT.	8.VII.		spent one night in billets at ALBERT.	W.P.

T2134. Wt. W708—776. 500000. 4/15. Sir J. C. & S.

Army Form C. 2118.

Instructions regarding War Diaries and Intelligence Summaries are contained in F. S. Regs., Part II. and the Staff Manual respectively. Title pages will be prepared in manuscript.

WAR DIARY
~~or~~
~~INTELLIGENCE~~ SUMMARY.

(*Erase heading not required.*)

Place	Date	Hour	Summary of Events and Information	Remarks and references to Appendices
BECOURT WOOD AND TRENCHES.	10.VII 11th		See Appendix B. report on the attack and capture of CONTALMAISON	Appendix "B." [illegible]
ALBERT.	12.VII		Coy relieved in CONTALMAISON by NO I. Coy. at 9. p.m. the sections arrived to our bivouacs near DERNANCOURT between 11. p.m. and 5.30. A.M. except 2 guns of no 2 section who were not relieved.	[illegible]
FRANVILLERS	13.VII		Rested one night at FRANVILLERS.	[illegible]
MOLLIENS aux BOIS.	14.VII		Bgde inspected in Fatigue dress by G.O.C. 23rd Division and complimented by him on their capture of CONTALMAISON.	
MOLLIENS etc	15.VII		Bgde inspected in drill order by G.O.C. IIIrd Corps. 2/Lt C.A.L. Saunders joined from Machine Gun Corps Base Depot.	[illegible]
MOLLIENS etc	16.VII		Company attended Divine service at Brigade Headquarters. G.O.C. 23rd Division present.	[illegible]
MOLLIENS etc	17.VII		2/Lt F.B. Marsh and 2/Lt G. Lindsay joined for duty from Machine Gun Corps Base Depot.	[illegible]
MOLLIENS	18.VII		No 13409 Pte Baines of 9th Yorkshire Regiment attached 69th Coy M.G.C and 5626 Pte Collins of awarded Military Medal. Ribbons presented by G.O.C 23rd Division.	[illegible]
MOLLIENS.	19.VII		Rest billets.	[illegible]

Instructions regarding War Diaries and Intelligence Summaries are contained in F. S. Regs., Part II. and the Staff Manual respectively. Title pages will be prepared in manuscript.

WAR DIARY

or

INTELLIGENCE SUMMARY.

(Erase heading not required.)

Army Form C. 2118.

Place	Date	Hour	Summary of Events and Information	Remarks and references to Appendices
MOLLIENS	20.VII		Rest billets. 55962 Pte Lewis J awarded Military Medal: ribbon presented by G.O.C. Division.	J.W.H.T.
MILLENCOURT	21.VII		Company marched to bivouacs at MILLENCOURT. 10.0 a.m.	J.W.H.T.
MILLENCOURT	22.VII		2/Lt G. W. Symes proceeded on a reconnaissance to CONTALMAISON and MAMETZ WOOD.	J.W.H.T.
MILLENCOURT	23.VII		Lieut. C.F.T. Baker and 5 other ranks proceeded to Machine Gun Course at CAMIERS.	J.W.H.T.
MILLENCOURT	24.VII		Company remained at MILLENCOURT.	J.W.H.T.
MILLENCOURT	25.VII		2/Lt L. d'Hautman de Villiers accidentally injured: evacuated to C.C.S.	J.W.H.T.
ALBERT.	26.VII		Company marched to billets in ALBERT: 8.45 a.m. Brigade in Divisional reserve.	J.W.H.T.
ALBERT.	27.VII		Company remained in reserve. 2/Lt H.S.C. Mead proceeded to reconnoitre trenches S.W. of MARTINPUICH.	J.W.H.T.
Trenches S. of MARTINPUICH	28.VII		Company relieved 68th M.G.C. in line. No 1 Section in front line. 10 guns in CONTALMAISON in support: 2 guns No 2 Section in reserve in HORSESHOE TRENCH. 2/Lt C. A. Saunders transferred to 70th M.G.C.	J.W.H.T.
Trenches S. of MARTINPUICH	29.VII		Casualties No 1 Section 1 other rank killed 1 O.R. wounded. 3 guns No 2 Section moved up into front line. Guns co-operated in attack by 10th Bn Duke of Wellington's Regiment on MUNSTER ALLEY. 8 guns 5th Cavalry M.G. Squadron attached for rations.	J.W.H.T.
Trenches S. of MARTINPUICH	30.VII		No 1 Section relieved by 2 guns No 3 Section and 2 guns No 4 Section. Gas shell and tear shells bombardment of CONTALMAISON.	J.W.H.T.
Trenches S. of MARTINPUICH	31.VII		Casualties due to gas poisoning. 1 Officer (Captain W.M.H. Pollen) 5 other ranks wounded.	J.W.H.T.

Army Form C. 2118.

WAR DIARY
or
INTELLIGENCE SUMMARY.
(Erase heading not required.)

Instructions regarding War Diaries and Intelligence Summaries are contained in F. S. Regs., Part II. and the Staff Manual, respectively. Title pages will be prepared in manuscript.

Place	Date	Hour	Summary of Events and Information	Remarks and references to Appendices
ALBERT.	1.VIII.		Company relieved by 68th Coy. M.G.C. Marched to billets in ALBERT: divisional reserve.	JMWT.
			War Diary completed up to 31 · VIII · 16.	
			J M W Toynbee Lt. Comdg 69th Coy M.G.C.	
			1/VIII	

T2134. Wt. W708—776. 500000. 4/15. Sir J. C. & S.

Copy Appendix A.

Report on operations carried out from 3rd to the 6th inst.

On the night of the 3rd instant I received orders to send 4 guns up to the SCOTTS REDOUBT Line. I took No 1 Section up and relieved the 101st by M.G.C. I left LIEUT. BAKER in charge of this section. LIEUT BAKER co-operated in a bombing raid which was made by the 11th West Yorkshire Regiment. He took one gun up the sap from which the Bombers had been driven back. During the 2nd Bombing raid LIEUT. BAKER'S guns gave covering fire. O.C. 11th WEST Yorks reported to me that LIEUT BAKER and LIEUT. RIGBY behaved remarkably well and were of great assistance to him. On the morning of the 5th instant at 4 a.m. I was ordered to send up two guns to be at the disposal of the 10th W. Riding Regiment – 2/Lieut SYMES was in charge of this party and assisted a working raid with covering fire. On the afternoon of the 5th I received orders to send all my guns up to SCOTS REDOUBT. These guns were distributed along the line from which the attack was made on the HORSESHOE Line – after the capture of this line I selected positions for guns in the new line and sent up 2 guns into it at the request of O.C. 8th Yorkshire Regiment. On the night of the 5th–6th Lieut BAKERS gun teams lost 6 men. The total casualties during this period were 2 officers and 15 other ranks. All the men behaved well and did useful work throughout the operations.

7/VII/16

(Signed) Walter H Potter Capt
Comd, 69th Coy M-G C.

Copy 1 Appendix B

Report on the Operations carried out at CONTALMAISON on the 10th–11th July 1916.

At 9.45 A.M. on the 10th inst in accordance with the G.O.C's orders I dispatched 2 guns under 2/Lt GRAVES from Albert with orders to proceed to the Front line & take up positions at about X 15 B. 8 0 and X 15 B. 8½

At 3.10 P.M. 2/Lt GRAVES brought one of his guns into action against a party of about 200 Germans who were attacking the line on our left on the next Brigade front.

The gun fired about 2 belts & the enemy retired to their own trenches. This gun fired from a position at X 15 B 7. 3.

At 4.20 p.m. both guns were in position as ordered. They opened fire on CONTALMAISON WOOD and trenches E & W of it. Also fired on parties of Germans seen retiring up the Valley towards POSIERES at about 6 p.m. and 7 p.m.

Enemy were also seen moving along the crest line E of POSIERES at 7.15 p.m & were dispersed by fire from these two guns. These guns fired almost continuously throughout the attack and had some very good targets

2/Lt GRAVES was in the same position with his guns until 10.30 AM on the 12th inst.

Two guns under 2/Lt SYMES were dispatched from ALBERT at 9.45 AM with orders to take up positions at the junction of SHELTER TRENCH and PEARL ALLEY to fire upon + enfilade the enemy's trench running thro' W edge of the village. These guns were in position at 4.0 pm. These guns fired about 5000 rounds between 4.20 and 5.10 p.m. and at 5.20 pm. they again fired on a party of 40 Germans retiring N E into the village causing heavy casualties.
At 9.0 pm. these guns advanced to front lines N of village with the consolidating party of the W. RIDING Regt. From new positions they fired on a small party of the enemy retreating W just before dawn. These guns were relieved at 10 p.m. on the 11th inst.

2/Lt Brutton with 4 guns ALBERT at 10.30 AM on the 10th inst + took up positions in BIRCH TREE WOOD at 12.30 pm.
These guns fired on the CUTTING continuously from 4.40 to 6.30 pm.
I gave 2/Lt BROTTON orders not to fire

after 6 30 p m in order to leave a margin of safety for the attacking troops. Two of these guns fired during the attack at parties of the enemy seen passing to and from X16 D 8 4 and X16 D 9. 2 The fire of all these guns was observed with glasses quite clearly from BIRCH TREE WOOD and considerable casualties were inflicted on the enemy by them

2/Lt BAKER with the 6 remaining guns remained at WILLOW PATCH from 3.30 pm until receiving orders from G O C. to bring guns up to H. Qrs at 6.10/pm the guns arrived at Hd Qs at about 8. 0 pm. and were despatched to CONTALMAISON where they took up position for 2 guns to fire NE of village + 2 guns to fire N of village, and on CONTALMAISON WOOD They were heavily shelled on their way up SHELTER ALLEY 2 guns were left at Hd Qrs at the disposal of G O C.

The men behaved in a most exemplary manner + were very keen to get their guns into action which they did with great success.

I cannot speak too highly of the behaviour

4

of the Officers & men, particularly 2/LT GRAVES and his men and 2/LT SYMES and his men.
The others did equally well though they did not have the same opportunities.

SIGNED

Walter H. Pollen
CAPT
Commdg 69th Coy M.G.C

69th Brigade

23rd Division.

69th BRIGADE

MACHINE GUN COMPANY

AUGUST 1 9 1 6

69 M G Coy

Army Form C. 2118.

Vol 7

Instructions regarding War Diaries and Intelligence Summaries are contained in F. S. Regs., Part II. and the Staff Manual respectively. Title pages will be prepared in manuscript.

WAR DIARY

~~or INTELLIGENCE SUMMARY.~~

(Erase heading not required.)

Place	Date	Hour	Summary of Events and Information	Remarks and references to Appendices
ALBERT	Aug 1st		Company relieved by 68th Coy M.G.C.: marched into billets in ALBERT: divisional reserve.	J.M.T.
ALBERT	Aug 2nd		Company remained in divisional reserve. 5617 L/Cpl Palmer W awarded Military Medal and ribbon presented by G.O.C 23rd Division.	J.M.T.
ALBERT	Aug 3rd		Brigade remained in divisional reserve: company remained in ALBERT.	J.M.T.
ALBERT	Aug 4th		NO change.	J.M.T.
Trenches S.W. of MARTINPUICH S W of MARTINPUICH	Aug 5th		Company relieved 68th Coy M.G.C in trenches S.W. of MARTINPUICH. 3 guns in GLOSTER ALLEY under 2/Lt MEAD: 2 guns in O.G 2 1 left, 1 right of MUNSTER ALLEY. 1 in new trench from the HOOK to MUNSTER ALLEY under 2/Lt BRUTTON and 2/Lt LINDSAY.	J.M.T.
Trenches S.W. of MARTINPUICH	Aug 6th		Company remained in trenches. 8th Bn Yorkshire Regiment made a successful bombing attack up MUNSTER ALLEY. About 5.30 pm order received from Brigade to send 2 guns up to GLOSTER ALLEY to prepare for attack on SWITCH LINE. Guns went up under 2/Lt SYMES: attack postponed: 2 guns went into the HOOK. All night 6th/7th heavy bombardment of O.G. 2. On one gun left of MUNSTER ALLEY Cpl Sherwood and 1 man were wounded: 1 wounded and missing and 5 were killed. Gun and tripod salvaged by 2/Lt GRAVES.	J.M.T.

T2134. Wt. W708—776. 500000. 4/15. Sir J. C. & S.

Instructions regarding War Diaries and Intelligence Summaries are contained in F. S. Regs., Part II. and the Staff Manual respectively. Title pages will be prepared in manuscript.

WAR DIARY
or
INTELLIGENCE SUMMARY.
(Erase heading not required.)

Army Form C. 2118.

Place	Date	Hour	Summary of Events and Information	Remarks and references to Appendices
Trenches and BRESLE	Aug. 7		Company relieved by 45th Coy M.G.C. Marched by sections to transport lines in BECOURT WOOD and marched from there to bivouac at BRESLE	JMcC
BRESLE	Aug. 8		Company remained at BRESLE. 69th Brigade marched into BRESLE	MMT.
BRESLE	Aug. 9		Company remained at BRESLE.	MMT.
BRESLE	Aug. 10		Captain H.G.V. Roberts joined for duty and assumed command of company. Transport moved with remainder of Brigade Transport at 3.0 pm to march to VAUCHELLES. Remainder of Company marched to entrain at MERICOURT: paraded 10.0 pm.	
VAUCHELLES	Aug. 11		Company entrained at MERICOURT 2.10 a.m.; detrained at PONT REMY 9.30 a.m.; marched to billets at VAUCHELLES-LES-QUESNOY.	MMT.
VAUCHELLES	Aug. 12		Company remained at VAUCHELLES.	MMT.
VAUCHELLES BAILLEUL.	Aug. 13		Company entrained at PONT REMY at 11.18 a.m. Detained at BAILLEUL 9.30 pm. Company now in V Corps.	
R31 X1	Aug. 14		Company remained in billets about R 31 and X1 north west of BAILLEUL.	MMT.
TROIS ARBRES	Aug. 15		Company moved to Transport lines of 122nd Coy M.G.C. at TROIS ARBRES near	

T2134. Wt. W708—776. 500000. 4/15. Sir J. C. & S.

Instructions regarding War Diaries and Intelligence Summaries are contained in F. S. Regs., Part II. and the Staff Manual respectively. Title pages will be prepared in manuscript.

WAR DIARY
or
INTELLIGENCE SUMMARY.
(Erase heading not required.)

Army Form C. 2118.

Place	Date	Hour	Summary of Events and Information	Remarks and references to Appendices
TROIS ARBRES	15.8.16		STEENWERCK	JMT.
PLOEGSTEERT	16.8.16		The company relieved 122nd Company M.G.C. in the line at PLOEGSTEERT. 10 guns in the line. 3 guns No 1, 3 guns No 2, 2 guns No 3, 2 guns No 4. Officers 2/Lt SYMES, 2/Lt BRUTTON, 2/Lt LINDSAY. Headquarters at U21 a 4:2. 2/Lt Lindsay i/c A Group, 2/Lt SYMES i/c B Group, 2/Lt BRUTTON i/c C Group. Working party dispersed by B1 gun and two working parties dispersed by A1 gun.	JMT.
PLOEGSTEERT	17.8.16		Enemy Machine Guns and Snipers active. Letter A3 gun fired 2000 rounds at enemy dumps and headquarters at TROIS TILLEULS FARM and SUGAR REFINERY.	JMT.
PLOEGSTEERT	18.8.16		Enemy machine guns and snipers active. Enemy shelled emplacement of B2 gun. Enemy transport heard entering MESSINES.	JMT.
PLOEGSTEERT	19.8.16		No firing on account of large working parties. Weather clear still and light. Enemy transport again heard entering MESSINES.	JMT.
PLOEGSTEERT	20.8.16		Situation continued normal. No firing by guns of the company. Enemy machine guns moderately active.	JMT.

T2134. Wt. W708—776. 500000. 4/15. Sir J. C. & S.

Instructions regarding War Diaries and Intelligence Summaries are contained in F. S. Regs., Part II. and the Staff Manual respectively. Title pages will be prepared in manuscript.

WAR DIARY
or
~~INTELLIGENCE SUMMARY.~~
(Erase heading not required.)

Army Form C. 2118.

Place	Date	Hour	Summary of Events and Information	Remarks and references to Appendices
PLOEGSTEERT	21.8.16		No firing from any of the company's guns – Enemy seen fetching water from a house in MESSINES – Enemy machine gun and rifle fire active during the night –	J. W. H. T.
PLOEGSTEERT	22.8.16.		Letter 'A' 1 gun fired 200 rounds at the flashes of enemy Machine Gun firing from U15d 95:40 – No results were apparent – Enemy machine guns were active throughout the night –	J.W.H.T.
PLOEGSTEERT	23.8.16.		About 300 rounds were fired from a position at U14b 75:50 for the purpose of ranging for future night firing, at houses in MESSINES where enemy had been seen moving about – Enemy retaliated with about 15 77mm shells slightly wounding 2/Lt E.W. BRUTTON.	J.W.H.T.
PLOEGSTEERT	24.8.16.		Situation normal: no firing by guns of the company –	J. W. H. T.
PLOEGSTEERT.	25.8.16.		69th Infantry Brigade relieved 70th Infantry Brigade in the line and took over the line from T112 to T127. The company relieved 5 guns of 70th Coy M. G. C. which were holding the line taken over by 69th Infantry Brigade. One one gun being withdrawn the company was left with 14 guns in the line.	J.W.H.T.

T2134. Wt. W708–776. 500000. 4/15. Sir J. C. & S.

Army Form C. 2118.

Instructions regarding War Diaries and Intelligence Summaries are contained in F. S. Regs., Part II. and the Staff Manual respectively. Title pages will be prepared in manuscript.

WAR DIARY
or
INTELLIGENCE SUMMARY.

(Erase heading not required.)

Place	Date	Hour	Summary of Events and Information	Remarks and references to Appendices
PLOEGSTEERT	26.8.16		Situation normal. No firing by guns of the company –	JMMT.
PLOEGSTEERT	27.8.16		Situation Quiet. No firing by guns of the company – Enemy observed bringing up large quantities of timber and making a considerable work at U15d 80 50.	JMMT.
PLOEGSTEERT	28.8.16		Situation quiet. No firing by our guns – Enemy machine gun position located at U22c 30 75 and U22c 34 54.	JMMT.
PLOEGSTEERT	29.8.16		Situation Quiet – No firing by our guns.	JMMT.
PLOEGSTEERT	30.8.16		Situation Quiet – A gun of the company firing from T120 (temporary position) fired about 300 rounds on a position in NO MANS LAND reported by patrol to be occupied by the enemy –	JMMT.
PLOEGSTEERT	31.8.16		Gas attack delivered on IX Corps front at 1.30 am. See appendix 'A'.	JMMT.
PLOEGSTEERT	1.9.16		War Diary for August 1916 completed	JMMT.

H.A. Roberts [illegible]
OC 69 [illegible]

T2134. Wt W708—776. 500000. 4/15. Sir J. C. & S.

No 69 Coy M Gun Corps Appendix A.

Report for 24 hours ending 31-8-16

OPERATIONS:—

Machine Guns of the company co-operated in the GAS ATTACK at 1.30 AM 31-8-16

One gun fired at BIRDCAGE from 1.35 to 2.10 AM from U21.d. 4:7. At 2.0 am the gun moved to U21.d.5:6. and fired on Square U.22.b. engaging an hostile gun in that area. This gun fired about 3000 rounds.

One gun fired at BIRDCAGE from 1.35 to 2.10 am from U.15.d.55:30 and at 2 am fired at FACTORY FARM and engaged and silenced an enemy gun firing from U b 55:40 This gun fired about 3000 rounds

Both the above guns at intervals were able to bring fire to bear on enemy seen moving in his trenches at points where the artillery bombardment had broken down the parapet.

One gun was also situated at about U21. b 15:60. as a reserve in case of necessity. This gun only fired about 200 rounds

at the machine gun already mentioned in company intelligence at U21. b. 7:3.

One gun also throughout the operations fired 1000 rounds in short bursts at TROIS TILLEULS FARM from a position at about U.15.c.60:55.

[illegible]

Instructions regarding War Diaries and Intelligence Summaries are contained in F. S. Regs., Part II. and the Staff Manual respectively. Title pages will be prepared in manuscript.

WAR DIARY

~~or~~

~~INTELLIGENCE SUMMARY.~~

(Erase heading not required.)

Army Form C. 2118.

Vol 8

69 MGC

Place	Date	Hour	Summary of Events and Information	Remarks and references to Appendices
PLOEGSTEERT	Sept. 1		Company remained in trenches in PLOEGSTEERT. Gas alarm about 11.0 pm but cancelled 15 minutes later. One gun fired 2750 rounds from Trench 119 and caused an enemy machine gun in the Birdcage to alter his position. Another gun firing from Trench S3 (WESTMINSTER Avenue) fired 4000 rounds at PONT ROUGE and dumps in the vicinity.	J.W.T.
PLOEGSTEERT	Sept. 2		Company remained in trenches. Situation quiet. No firing by our guns.	J.W.T.
PLOEGSTEERT	Sept. 3		Company remained in trenches. Situation quiet. No firing by our guns.	J.W.H.T.
PLOEGSTEERT	Sept. 4		Company relieved by 56th Company Machine Gun Corps. Company marched to camp at 2nd A.N.Z.A.C. Training area S27 b. (Map: 28. S.W.)	J.W.H.T.
S27 b.	Sept. 5		Company remained in Camp at S27 b. (Map 28 S.W.)	J.W.T.
BAILLEUL ST OMER PETIT DIFQUES	Sept. 6		Company marched to BAILLEUL and entrained at 11.28 am for ST OMER. Detrained at ST OMER at 12.45 pm and marched to billets at PETIT DIFQUES.	J.W.H.T.
PETIT DIFQUES	Sept. 7		Company remained in billets at PETIT DIFQUES.	J.W.T.
PETIT DIFQUES	Sept. 8		Company remained in billets at PETIT DIFQUES. Attached men all fired at	

Instructions regarding War Diaries and Intelligence Summaries are contained in F. S. Regs., Part II. and the Staff Manual respectively. Title pages will be prepared in manuscript.

WAR DIARY
or
~~INTELLIGENCE SUMMARY~~.
(Erase heading not required.)

Army Form C. 2118.

Place	Date	Hour	Summary of Events and Information	Remarks and references to Appendices
PETIT DIFQUES	Sept 8		thirty yards range. Advanced party under 2 Lt G. W. SYMES proceeded to AMIENS.	MMT.
PETIT DIFQUES	Sept 9		Inspection of company in all branches of work including firing.	MMT.
PETIT DIFQUES	Sept 10.		Company marched to AUDRUICK Station and entrained for LONGUEAU at 7.39 p.m.	MMT.
LONGUEAU POULAINVILLE	Sept 11		Company detrained at LONGUEAU about 5.0 a.m. and marched to billets at POULAINVILLE.	MMT.
POULAINVILLE HENENCOURT WOOD	Sept 12		Company, moving with Brigade marched to HENENCOURT WOOD, VIA COISY and BAIZIEUX. Company was billeted in huts in HENENCOURT WOOD.	MMT.
HENENCOURT WOOD.	Sept 13		Company remained in billets at HENENCOURT WOOD.	MMT.
HENENCOURT WOOD	Sept 14		Company remained in billets at HENENCOURT WOOD. Tactical exercise was carried out on 69th Brigade training area.	MMT.
HENENCOURT WOOD MILLENCOURT	Sept 15 Sept 16 Sept 17		Tactical exercise carried out on 69th Brigade training area. Company moved to billets at MILLENCOURT. Company remained at MILLENCOURT.	MMT.
MARTINPUICH	Sept 18		Company relieved 44th M. G. C. in MARTINPUICH sector & during next 24	

T2134. Wt. W708—776. 500000. 4/15. Sir J. C. & S.

Instructions regarding War Diaries and Intelligence Summaries are contained in F. S. Regs., Part II. and the Staff Manual respectively. Title pages will be prepared in manuscript.

WAR DIARY
or
INTELLIGENCE SUMMARY.
(Erase heading not required.)

Army Form C. 2118.

Place	Date	Hour	Summary of Events and Information	Remarks and references to Appendices
MARTINPUICH	Sept 8th		[illegible] took over 800 yards on the E of MARTINPUICH from 150 M.G.C.	AHG.
MARTINPUICH	Sept 19th		Company in trenches in MARTINPUICH section. For operations in this period see Appendix "A"	AHG See Appendix "A"
MARTINPUICH	Sept 20th			AHG
MARTINPUICH	Sept 21st			AHG
MARTINPUICH	Sept 22nd		Company relieved by 68 M.G.C at 10.0 am; relief complete by 1.0 pm; and	AHG
LONELY TRENCH	Sept 22nd		company moved back to Reserve at LONELY TRENCH taking over from 70 M.G.C	AHG
LONELY TRENCH	Sept 23rd		Company remained in Divisional Reserve in LONELY TRENCH.	AHG
LONELY TRENCH	Sept 24th			AHG
LONELY TRENCH	Sept 25th			AHG
CONTALMAISON	Sept 26th		Company relieved 70 M.G.C and moved up to Divisional Support in CONTALMAISON, one section remaining at LONELY TRENCH. Work done on dugouts and shelters.	AHG.
CONTALMAISON	Sept 27th		Company remained in CONTALMAISON. MILITARY MEDAL awarded by CORPS COMMANDER to 5589 Sgt J. Cain, 6242 L/c G. McDine, 5636 Pte H. Wakeling, 23125 Pte T. Bowman.	AHG.

T2134. Wt. W708—776. 500000. 4/15. Sir J. C. & S.

Instructions regarding War Diaries and Intelligence Summaries are contained in F. S. Regs., Part II. and the Staff Manual respectively. Title pages will be prepared in manuscript.

WAR DIARY

~~or INTELLIGENCE SUMMARY.~~

(Erase heading not required.)

Army Form C. 2118.

Place	Date	Hour	Summary of Events and Information	Remarks and references to Appendices
CONTALMAISON	Sept 28th		Presentation of MILITARY MEDAL by G.O.C. 23rd Division. Company remained in CONTALMAISON. Work continued on dugouts and shelters.	AHG
CONTALMAISON	Sept 29th		Company remained in CONTALMAISON. Work continued as above.	
CONTALMAISON	Sept 30th			AHG.
CONTALMAISON.	Oct: 1st		War diary for September 1st Completed.	JW

H. G. Robertson Capt
OC 69 Coy

T2134. Wt. W708—776. 500000. 4/15. Sir J. C. & S.

To/

Staff Captain

69th Infantry Brigade

Attached herewith please find War Diary in Duplicate for the month of October 1916.

B 62.
3/11/16

J. G. Roberts
Captain

Commdg. No. 69 M. G. Coy

Instructions regarding War Diaries and Intelligence Summaries are contained in F. S. Regs., Part II. and the Staff Manual respectively. Title pages will be prepared in manuscript.

WAR DIARY
or
~~INTELLIGENCE SUMMARY~~.
(Erase heading not required.)

Vol 9

Army Form C. 2118.

Place	Date	Hour	Summary of Events and Information	Remarks and references to Appendices
CONTALMAISON	October 1st		Company remained in dugouts at CONTALMAISON	AHG
LE SARS.	October 2nd		Company relieved 70 M.G.C into trenches in front of LE SARS. Relief complete by 10.0 p.m.	AHG
LE SARS	October 3rd		— Military Medal awarded 8177 Pte W. Brown by CORPS COMMANDER	AHG.
LE SARS	October 4th			Vide AHG.
LE SARS	October 5th		Operations at LE SARS. Vide Appendix.	Appendix AHG.
LE SARS	October 6th			AHG.
LE SARS	October 7th			AHG.
LE SARS	October 8th		Company relieved by 45 M.G.C.	AHG
LONELY TRENCH / ALBERT	October 9th		On relief company moved back to LONELY TRENCH and marched into ALBERT arriving in billets at 3.0 p.m. Company bathe at 4.30 p.m.	AHG
ALBERT	October 10th		Company remained in billets at ALBERT. ~~The~~ 69th Brigade inspected by CORPS COMMANDER at 9.30 a.m.	AHG.
ALBERT	October 11th		Company remained in billets in ALBERT. Advanced billeting party entrained for POPERINGHE at MERICOURT Station at 11.0 a.m. Brigade transport left ALBERT by ~~R~~ road for VAUCHELLE.	

T2134. Wt. W708—776. 500000. 4/15. Sir J. C. & S.

Instructions regarding War Diaries and Intelligence Summaries are contained in F. S. Regs., Part II. and the Staff Manual respectively. Title pages will be prepared in manuscript.

WAR DIARY

~~or~~

~~INTELLIGENCE SUMMARY.~~

(Erase heading not required.)

Army Form C. 2118.

Place	Date	Hour	Summary of Events and Information	Remarks and references to Appendices
ALBERT & YVRENCHEUX	October 12th		Company entrained by tactical train about 9.0 p.m.	AHG.
YVRENCHEUX	October 13th		Company detrained at LONGPRE-LES-CORPS-SAINTS about 7.0 p.m. and proceeded by motor lorries to billets at YVRENCHEUX arriving at 10.0 p.m.	AHG.
YVRENCHEUX	October 14th		Company at YVRENCHEUX. MILITARY MEDAL awarded by CORPS COMMANDER to 23127 Sgt Cowling, 23124 Cpl Camb, 23133 L/C Hoggard E, 18715 Pte Banaclough H.	
			~~At 11.57 pm~~ Company entrained for POPERINGHE by sections at 3 hour intervals, Head quarters & one section at 11.57 p.m.	AHG
POPERINGHE	October 15th		Company arrived at POPERINGHE, Head quarters & one section detraining at 6.0 am the remaining sections at 3 hour intervals, at HOPOUTRE Station. Marched to billets in the RUE D'YPRES.	AHG.
POPERINGHE	October 16th		Company remained in billets in POPERINGHE	AHG.
POPERINGHE	October 17th		Presentation of MILITARY MEDAL by G.O.C. 23rd DIVISION at 2.30 p.m. to 23127 Sgt Cowling H, 23124 Cpl Camb, 23133 L/C Hoggard E, 18715 Pte Banaclough H. Company remained in billets.	AHG.
POPERINGHE	October 18th		Company remained in billets in POPERINGHE.	AHG.

T2134. Wt. W708-776. 500000. 4/15. Sir J. C. & S.

Army Form C. 2118.

WAR DIARY

or

~~INTELLIGENCE SUMMARY.~~

(Erase heading not required.)

Instructions regarding War Diaries and Intelligence Summaries are contained in F. S. Regs., Part II. and the Staff Manual respectively. Title pages will be prepared in manuscript.

Place	Date	Hour	Summary of Events and Information	Remarks and references to Appendices
POPERINGHE	October 19th		Company remained in billets in POPERINGHE.	AHG
POPERINGHE	October 20th		Company remained in billets in POPERINGHE	AHG.
POPERINGHE	October 21st		Company remained in billets in POPERINGHE	AHG.
POPERINGHE	October 22nd		Company remained in billets in POPERINGHE. MILITARY MEDAL awarded by CORPS COMMANDER to 8902 Sgt Manning G., 9602 a/Cpl Spivey N., 8397 L/C Leeson J. H., 5612 Pte Standell W., 42333 Pte Whitton J.	AHG.
ZILLEBEKE	October 23rd		Company relieved 68 M.G.C. in the left sector of the Divisional front, entraining at POPERINGHE at 7 p.m. and detraining at YPRES 7.45 p.m. Owing to guides losing their way, relief was not complete till 2.30 a.m. 24/10/16.	AHG
ZILLEBEKE	October 24th		Company in trenches between HOOGE ROAD and ZILLEBEKE. Dispositions Company Headquarters Capt H.G.V. ROBERTS, Lt AHGRAVES and 3 guns AHG in reserve at ZILLEBEKE BUND: in the line 9 guns — 2 guns under 2/Lt G. LINDSAY at YEOMANRY POST, positions approximately I 17 d 3.3 and I 24 a 2.7 (Ref Sheet 28 N.W. Ed 3.D.) — 2 guns under 2/Lt M. J. DAWSON at ZILLEBEKE I 22 b 9.3 and DORMY HOUSE I 23 a 7.6 — 5 guns on the left under 2/Lt B.S. TIERNEY	

2353 Wt. W2544/1454 700,000 5/15 D. D. & L. A.D.S.S./Forms/C. 2118.

Instructions regarding War Diaries and Intelligence Summaries are contained in F. S. Regs., Part II. and the Staff Manual respectively. Title pages will be prepared in manuscript.

WAR DIARY

or

~~INTELLIGENCE SUMMARY~~.

(Erase heading not required.)

Army Form C. 2118.

Place	Date	Hour	Summary of Events and Information	Remarks and references to Appendices
ZILLEBEKE	October 24th		at HALFWAY HOUSE, approximate positions – GORDON HOUSE I 16 b 30.25, CHINA WALL I 16 b 65.00, HALF WAY HOUSE I 17 c 20.85, LEINSTER FARM I 17 a 95.25, and RUINED HOUSE I 17 d 95.90 – In YPRES one section and untrained attached men: training carried out under 2/Lt G. W. SYMES at 160 RUE DE LILLE. Transport remained in POPERINGHE.	AHG.
ZILLEBEKE	October 25th		Company remained in trenches: work on dugouts and emplacements.	AHG.
ZILLEBEKE	October 26th		Company remained in trenches: work continued as above.	AHG.
ZILLEBEKE	October 27th		Company remained in trenches: new emplacement reconnoitred for CHINAWALL gun at about I 16 b 80.10	AHG.
ZILLEBEKE	October 28th		Company remained in trenches: MILITARY MEDAL presented by G.O.C. to 8902 Sgt HANNING. G 9602 L/Cpl SPIVEY N, 8391 L/C LEESON J. H, 5612 Pte STANDELL W at Infantry Barracks, YPRES: Three gun teams moved up from YPRES to dugouts at ZILLEBEKE BUND: work commenced on emplacement and dugout in front line at I 17 b 70.25	AHG.
ZILLEBEKE	October 29th		~~CHINA WALL~~ gun AHG Company remained in trenches, ~~[illegible]~~ RUINED HOUSE AHG gun	

2353 Wt. W2544/1454 700,000 5/15 D. D. & L. A.D.S.S./Forms/C. 2118.

Army Form C. 2118.

Instructions regarding War Diaries and Intelligence Summaries are contained in F. S. Regs., Part II. and the Staff Manual respectively. Title pages will be prepared in manuscript.

WAR DIARY
or
~~INTELLIGENCE SUMMARY.~~
(Erase heading not required.)

Place	Date	Hour	Summary of Events and Information	Remarks and references to Appendices
ZILLEBEKE	October 29th		moved to position prepared in front line I 17 b 70.25. Inter-section relief of gun teams complete by 7.15 p.m.	AHG.
ZILLEBEKE	October 30th		Company remained in trenches. Trench mortar activity on right of Divisional front between 1.0 pm and 6.0 pm.	AHG.
ZILLEBEKE	October 31st		Company remained in trenches. Work commenced on new dug-out at GORDON HOUSE. MILITARY CROSS awarded by C in C to 2/Lt G. W. SYMES	
			During period 23-10-16 – 31-10-16 situation remained quiet with occasional Trench mortar and artillery activity, chiefly on right sector of divisional front. No firing took place by any guns of the Company.	AHG.
ZILLEBEKE	November 1st		War Diary completed for October 1916.	AHG. For Defence Scheme See APPENDIX. AHG.

[signature] Capt.
OC 61 M.G.C.

2353 Wt. W2544/1454 700,000 5/15 D. D. & L. A.D.S.S./Forms/C. 2118.

APPENDIX.

69th M.G.C.

Outline of Defence Scheme Left Sector of Divisional Front YPRES. October 1916.

Map Belgium Sheet 28 NW

(1) Disposition of Guns.

Coy HQs ZILLEBEKE BUND. I 15 d 33

GROUP A. 1 officer HQ ZILLEBEKE.
No 1. Gun I 22 b 9 3 ZILLEBEKE GUN.
No 2 Gun I 23 a 6 6 DORMY HOUSE Gun
GROUP B. 1 officer HQs WELLINGTON CRESCENT.
No 1 Gun I 23 b 8580 YEOMANRY POST GUN
No 2 Gun I 17 d 4 2 ROSSLYN ST GUN.
GROUP C. 1 officer HQs HALFWAY HOUSE
No 1 Gun I 17 d 45 95 opposite RUINED Ho GUN
No 2 Gun I 17 a 9.3. LEINSTER Fm GUN
No 3 Gun I 17 c 25 75 HALFWAY Ho GUN.
No 4 Gun I 16 b 0.6 CHINA WALL GUN.
No 5 Gun I 16 b 5 4 GORDON Ho GUN.

All the above guns with the exception of A 1 (ZILLEBEKE) + C 3. (HALFWAY Ho) will in the event of hostile attack hold their position + fight to the last. Guns A1 + C3 are forward reserve guns + will be used as circumstances demand.

Instructions regarding War Diaries and Intelligence Summaries are contained in F. S. Regs., Part II. and the Staff Manual respectively. Title pages will be prepared in manuscript.

Army Form C. 2118.

WAR DIARY
or
~~INTELLIGENCE SUMMARY.~~
(Erase heading not required.)

69 Coy
MGC

REGISTRY MACHINE GUN CORPS 11 DEC 1916 RECORD OFFICE No. [illegible]

(141)

Place	Date	Hour	Summary of Events and Information	Remarks and references to Appendices
ZILLEBEKE	Nov 1st		Company remained in trenches. Work continued on GORDON HOUSE DUGOUT.	AHS
ZILLEBEKE	Nov 2nd		Company remained in trenches. Line strengthened in front of DORMY HOUSE CAMP. Work continued on GORDON HOUSE DUGOUT.	AHS
ZILLEBEKE	Nov 3rd		Company relieved by 70 M.G.C. Relief was complete by [illegible] p.m. On relief the Company marched to ERIE camp the last party arriving about 1.0 am 4/11/16. Transport remained in POPERINGHE. (10)	AHS AHG
ERIE CAMP	Nov 4th		Company in huts at ERIE CAMP	AHS
ERIE CAMP	Nov 5th		Company in huts at ERIE CAMP. Work continued on improvement of roads and huts.	AHS
ERIE CAMP	Nov 6th		Company in huts at ERIE CAMP. MILITARY CROSS presented to 2/Lt C. W. SYKES by G.O.C. 23rd DIVISION.	AHS
ERIE CAMP	Nov 7th		Company in huts at ERIE CAMP. Work continued on improvement of roads and huts.	AHS
ERIE CAMP	Nov 8th		Company in huts at ERIE CAMP	AHS
ERIE CAMP	Nov 9th		Company paraded at 3.0 pm at ERIE CAMP for relief of 68 M.G.C. in the right sector of the Divisional front. Relief complete by 10.0 pm.	AHS

2353 Wt. W2544/1454 700,000 5/15 D. D. & L. A.D.S.S./Forms/C. 2118.

Instructions regarding War Diaries and Intelligence Summaries are contained in F. S. Regs., Part II. and the Staff Manual respectively. Title pages will be prepared in manuscript.

WAR DIARY

or

~~INTELLIGENCE SUMMARY~~

(Erase heading not required.)

Army Form C. 2118.

(142)

Place	Date	Hour	Summary of Events and Information	Remarks and references to Appendices
ZILLEBEKE	November 9th		In the line – 9 guns: Forward group guns at HEDD STREET, REDAN HALIFAX STREET TUNNEL (Sty Hole) STAFFORD STREET (NORTH) STAFFORD STREET SOUTH RUDKIN HOUSE – under 2/Lt G. W. SYMES at HALIFAX STREET. Back group guns at VALLEY COTTAGE and SCHOOL HOUSE ZILLEBEKE under 2/Lt L. R. CALDWELL at ZILLEBEKE. At Head Quarters (BUND) 3 guns. At YPRES, 4 guns under 2/Lt M. S. DAWSON and untrained attached men.	
~~ZILLEBEKE~~				[illegible]
ZILLEBEKE	November 10th		Company remained in trenches. Situation quiet. Work carried out on TUNNEL and emplacements.	
ZILLEBEKE	November 11th		Company remained in trenches. Situation quiet. Work continued on TUNNEL and emplacements.	[illegible]
ZILLEBEKE	November 12th		Company remained in trenches. Situation quiet with the exception of French Minenwerfer activity between 3 pm and 6 pm. A [illegible] from [illegible] TUNNEL [illegible] and [illegible] YEOMANRY POST carried out in KLEIN ZILLEBEKE.	[illegible]
ZILLEBEKE	November ~~13th~~		Company remained in trenches. French mortar activity between 3 pm and 6 pm. Work continued on TUNNEL and new emplacements.	[illegible]

Instructions regarding War Diaries and Intelligence Summaries are contained in F. S. Regs., Part II. and the Staff Manual respectively. Title pages will be prepared in manuscript.

WAR DIARY
or
~~INTELLIGENCE~~ SUMMARY.
(Erase heading not required.)

Army Form C. 2118.

(143)

Place	Date	Hour	Summary of Events and Information	Remarks and references to Appendices
ZILLEBEKE	November 14th		Company remained in trenches. Firing carried out during afternoon on KLEIN ZILLEBEKE. Situation quiet. Work carried out on TUNNEL and new EMPLACEMENTS	A.H.S.
ZILLEBEKE	November 15th		Company remained in trenches. Situation quiet.	A.H.S.
ZILLEBEKE	November 16th		Company remained in trenches. Hostile Trench Mortar and artillery activity on OBSERVATORY RIDGE during afternoon. Work continued as above.	A.H.S.
ZILLEBEKE	November 17th		Company remained in trenches. Situation quiet. Firing carried out during afternoon on KLEIN ZILLEBEKE. Work continued on TUNNEL and new EMPLACEMENTS.	A.H.S.
ZILLEBEKE	November 18th		Company remained in trenches. 400 rounds fired on KLEIN ZILLEBEKE. Situation quiet. Work as usual.	A.H.S.
ZILLEBEKE	November 19th		Company remained in trenches. Situation quiet. Emplacement completed at S. end of BUND.	A.H.S.
ZILLEBEKE	November 20th		Company remained in trenches. Three emplacements and connecting trench completed 500x WEST of TRANSPORT FARM. Usual hostile Trench Mortar activity between 3 pm and 6 pm on OBSERVATORY RIDGE.	A.H.S.

2353 Wt. W2544/1454 700,000 5/15 D. D. & L. A.D.S.S./Forms/C. 2118.

Instructions regarding War Diaries and Intelligence Summaries are contained in F. S. Regs., Part II. and the Staff Manual respectively. Title pages will be prepared in manuscript.

WAR DIARY
or
~~INTELLIGENCE SUMMARY.~~
(Erase heading not required.)

Army Form C. 2118.

(144)

Place	Date	Hour	Summary of Events and Information	Remarks and references to Appendices
[illegible]	November 21st		Company relieved in the line by 70 M.G.C. Relief complete by 10. p.m. On relief Company marched to ERIE CAMP. Transport remained in POPERINGHE	A.M.S.
ERIE CAMP	November 22nd		Company in huts at ERIE CAMP	
ERIE CAMP	November 23rd		Company in huts at ERIE CAMP. Following extract from LONDON	
"			GAZETTE dated Nov. 23rd.	
			To be Temporary Lieutenants.....	
			2/Lt C.F.T. BAKER	
			Temp. 2/Lt M.S. DAWSON	
			Temp. 2/Lt C.W. SYMES	
			2/Lt B.S. TIERNEY "	
			Work commenced on new Transport lines at [illegible]	A.M.S.
ERIE CAMP	November 24th		Company in huts at ERIE CAMP. Work continued on new Transport lines	A.M.S.
ERIE CAMP	November 25th		Company in huts at ERIE CAMP. Work continued on new Transport lines	A.M.S.
ERIE CAMP	November 26th		Company in huts at ERIE CAMP. Captain H.C.V. ROBERTS [illegible] to England. GRANTHAM — authority [illegible] Telegram. Command of Company taken over by Lt TOYNBEE [illegible]	A.M.S.
ERIE CAMP	November 27th		Company in huts at ERIE CAMP. Lt B.S. TIERNEY [illegible] to [illegible]	

2353 Wt. W2544/1454 700,000 5/15 D. D. & L. A.D.S.S./Forms/C. 2118.

Army Form C. 2118.

Instructions regarding War Diaries and Intelligence Summaries are contained in F. S. Regs., Part II. and the Staff Manual respectively. Title pages will be prepared in manuscript.

WAR DIARY
or
INTELLIGENCE SUMMARY.

(Erase heading not required.)

(145)

Place	Date	Hour	Summary of Events and Information	Remarks and references to Appendices
ERIE CAMP	Nov	27th	M.S. / COLONIAL for duty with W.A.F.F. [illegible] Telegram 3096 A G q dated 20.11.16. Work continued on new Transport lines G 11 C 8.3 (Reference Sheet 28 N.W.)	AHS
ERIE CAMP	Nov	28th	Company relieved 68 M.G.C. in the left sector of the DIVISIONAL FRONT. Owing to a raid which was to have been carried out by the 55th DIVISION the relief was postponed for three hours and was therefore not complete till 1.30 a.m. 29/11/16. Disposition: In the line 9 guns: Right group 4 guns under 2/Lt L.R. CALDWELL at WELLINGTON CRESCENT – ZILLEBEKE – DORMY HOUSE, YEOMANRY POST, ROSLYN STREET: Left group 5 guns under 2/Lt H.S. DAWSON at HALF WAY HOUSE – GORDON HOUSE, CANAL WALL, HALF WAY HOUSE, LEINSTER FARM, FRONT LINE: H.Q. at BUND with 3 guns: 4 guns at MAISON DE POZIERES in YPRES under a/Capt Can[illegible]	AHS AHS
ZILLEBEKE	Nov	29th	Company remained in trenches. Situation quiet: about 1.0 p.m. 10 H.S. shells were fired at GORDON HOUSE. Work carried out on new dugouts at GORDON HOUSE and FORT (I 15 c 60.05 Ref Sheet 28 N.W.)	AHS

2353 Wt. W2544/1454 700,000 5/15 D. D. & L. A.D.S.S./Forms/C. 2118.

Army Form C. 2118.

Instructions regarding War Diaries and Intelligence Summaries are contained in F. S. Regs., Part II. and the Staff Manual respectively. Title pages will be prepared in manuscript.

WAR DIARY
or
~~INTELLIGENCE SUMMARY.~~
(Erase heading not required.)

(146)

Place	Date	Hour	Summary of Events and Information	Remarks and references to Appendices
ZILLEBEKE	Nov 30th		Company remained in trenches. Situation quiet. Work continued on NEW CORDON HOUSE DUGOUT and FORT. 2/Lt H WILSON + J ENTWISTLE reported for duty at H.Q.	
ZILLEBEKE	December 1st		War Diary completed for November [illegible].	[illegible]

J W H [illegible] Lieut
Comdg 69th Company MGC

2333 Wt. W2544/1454 700,000 5/15 D. D. & L. A.D.S.S./Forms/C. 2118.

Instructions regarding War Diaries and Intelligence Summaries are contained in F. S. Regs., Part II. and the Staff Manual respectively. Title pages will be prepared in manuscript.

WAR DIARY
or
~~INTELLIGENCE SUMMARY.~~
(Erase heading not required.)

Army Form C. 2118.

Vol XI
69th M.G. Coy.

Place	Date	Hour	Summary of Events and Information	Remarks and references to Appendices
ZILLEBEKE	December 1st		Company remained in trenches. Situation quiet. Work continued on NEW GORDON HOUSE DUG OUT and FORT.	AHS.
ZILLEBEKE	December 2nd		Company remained in trenches. Situation quiet. Intersection relief of teams in the line carried out. Work on new dugouts and emplacements continued.	AHS.
ZILLEBEKE	December 3rd		Company remained in trenches. Considerable H.T.M. activity on both sides on the right brigade front. Work continued on new dugouts and emplacements.	AHS.
ZILLEBEKE	December 4th		Company remained in trenches. ZILLEBEKE & DORMY HOUSE guns shelled but no damage. Usual Trench Mortar activity on right brigade front. Work continued on new dugouts and emplacements.	AHS.
ZILLEBEKE	December 5th		Company remained in trenches. During the afternoon artillery were active on both sides. 4.2s and 5.9s fell near DORMY HOUSE & GORDON HOUSE. The BUND was shelled and several casualties caused & damage done to NORTH SAKE duck boards. 500 rounds were fired ~~at 3~~ between 3 am & 3.30 am. from HALF WAY HOUSE on TRENCH TRAMWAY JUNCTION at HOOGE.	AHS.
ZILLEBEKE	December 6th		Company remained in trenches.	

2353 Wt. W2544/1454 700,000 5/15 D. D. & L. A.D.S.S./Forms/C. 2118.

Instructions regarding War Diaries and Intelligence Summaries are contained in F. S. Regs., Part II. and the Staff Manual respectively. Title pages will be prepared in manuscript.

WAR DIARY

or

~~INTELLIGENCE SUMMARY.~~

(Erase heading not required.)

Army Form C. 2118.

Place	Date	Hour	Summary of Events and Information	Remarks and references to Appendices
ZILLEBEKE	December 6th		Inter-Section relief of teams in the line. Work continued on GARDON HOUSE & YEOMANRY FORT DUGOUTS — Situation quiet	AHS.
ZILLEBEKE	December 7th		Company in trenches. Work continued as usual — situation quiet	AHS.
ZILLEBEKE	December 8th		Company remained in trenches. Usual H.T.M. activity on OBSERVATORY RIDGE. Our artillery retaliated with good results. Work continued as usual.	
ZILLEBEKE	December 9th		Company remained in trenches. Owing to mist there was very little artillery activity. During the night there was less machine gun fire than usual. Work continued.	AHS.
ZILLEBEKE	December 10th		Company remained in trenches. During the afternoon there was considerable artillery activity on both sides. ZILLEBEKE and ZILLEBEKE BUND were shelled with 4 H.V. Work continued as usual.	AHS.
ZILLEBEKE	December 11th		Company remained in trenches. Situation quiet. Intersection relief of gun teams carried out during the afternoon. Work continued as usual	AHS.
ZILLEBEKE	December 12th		Company remained in trenches. Situation quiet. Work continued as usual.	AHS.

2353 Wt. W2544/1454 700,000 5/15 D. D. & L. A.D.S.S./Forms/C. 2118.

Instructions regarding War Diaries and Intelligence Summaries are contained in F. S. Regs., Part II. and the Staff Manual respectively. Title pages will be prepared in manuscript.

WAR DIARY
or
~~INTELLIGENCE SUMMARY.~~
(Erase heading not required.)

Army Form C. 2118.

Place	Date	Hour	Summary of Events and Information	Remarks and references to Appendices
ZILLEBEKE	December 13th		Company remained in trenches. Enemy artillery active during the afternoon. ZILLEBEKE TERDON HOUSE were shelled with shrapnel & 4.2. Alternative emplacements constructed for FRONT LINE TTROISBYNN ST GUNS	A.A.S.
ZILLEBEKE	December 14th		Company relieved by 70 M. G. Coy. Relief complete by 10.45 pm. On relief company marched back to huts at ERIE CAMP	A.A.G.
ERIE CAMP ~~[illegible]~~	December 15th		Company remained in ~~[illegible]~~ A.A.G. huts at ERIE CAMP. During the morning and afternoon work was continued on new Transport Lines at G11 c 8.8	A.A.G.
ERIE CAMP	December 16th		Company remained in huts at ERIE CAMP. Working party found at 8.7.0 am. for drainage at G 14 b 4.9. ~~[illegible]~~ A.A.G. under R.E supervision. Work continued on new Transport Lines during morning and afternoon. Three men per section under Lt G.W. Symes fired Revolver Course at Brigade School ERIE CAMP. 56 OR. inoculated with T.A.B. vaccine	A.A.G.
ERIE CAMP	December 17th		Company remained in huts at ERIE. Captain H. Freeman from the Base assumed command of the Company with effect from this date. Work continued on transport lines during the morning. Three men per section paraded	

2353 Wt. W2544/1454 700,000 5/15 D. D. & L. A.D.S.S./Forms/C. 2118.

Army Form C. 2118.

WAR DIARY
or
~~INTELLIGENCE SUMMARY.~~
(Erase heading not required.)

Instructions regarding War Diaries and Intelligence Summaries are contained in F. S. Regs., Part II. and the Staff Manual respectively. Title pages will be prepared in manuscript.

Place	Date	Hour	Summary of Events and Information	Remarks and references to Appendices
ERIE CAMP.	December 17th		at 9 a.m. at Brigade School for instruction in bombing. Revolver practice continued. Revolvers issued to gun numbers in lieu of rifles and bayonets. Working party paraded at 3.45 p.m. for cable laying at ZILLEBEKE proceeding to YPRES by train.	A.H.G.
ERIE CAMP	December 18th		Company remained in ERIE CAMP. Work continued as above.	A.H.G.
ERIE CAMP	December 19th		Company remained in ERIE CAMP. Work continued as above.	A.H.G.
ERIE CAMP	December 20th		Company remained in ERIE CAMP. Work continued as above.	A.H.G.
ERIE CAMP	December 21st		Company remained in ERIE CAMP. Work continued as above.	A.H.G.
ERIE CAMP / ZILLEBEKE.	December 22nd		Company relieved 68 M.G. Coy in the right sector of the Divisional Front. Relief complete by 9.0 p.m. During the relief a raid was carried out by the 47th Division on our right. As no warning of this had been given, several casualties occurred to personnel and transport owing to enemy retaliation on ZILLEBEKE and communication trenches. Dispositions. In the line. 11 guns – Right sector under Lt A.H. Graves 4 guns at VALLEY COTTAGE, STAFFORD ST. NORTH, STAFFORD ST SOUTH and RUDKIN HOUSE: H.Q. RUDKIN TUNNEL – Middle Sector under Lt M. J. Dawson	

2353 Wt. W2544/1454 700,000 5/15 D. D. & L. A.D.S.S./Forms/C. 2118.

Army Form C. 2118.

Instructions regarding War Diaries and Intelligence Summaries are contained in F. S. Regs., Part II. and the Staff Manual respectively. Title pages will be prepared in manuscript.

WAR DIARY
or
INTELLIGENCE SUMMARY.
(Erase heading not required.)

Place	Date	Hour	Summary of Events and Information	Remarks and references to Appendices
			4 guns at SCHOOL HOUSE ZILLEBEKE, OBSERVATORY HOLE, DUMP HOLE and SPY HOLE: Left sector under Lt G.W. SYMES – 3 guns at HALIFAX STREET, REDAN, and HEDGE STREET H.Q. Middle & Left Sectors E. END of PETROGRAD SAP.	A.H.S.
ZILLEBEKE	December 23rd		Company remained in trenches. Work carried out on emplacements and dugouts.	A.H.S.
ZILLEBEKE	December 24th		Company remained in trenches. Work continued on as above. During the afternoon enemy artillery ~~[illegible]~~ was active on MOUNT SORREL and TOR TOP.	A.H.S.
ZILLEBEKE	December 25th		Company remained in trenches. Work continued as above. Situation quiet	A.H.S.
ZILLEBEKE	December 26th		Company remained in trenches. Intersection relief carried out in right sector. Considerable aeroplane activity on both sides. Alternative emplacements ~~[illegible]~~ AHS constructed at HALIFAX STREET and HEDGE STREET.	A.H.S.
ZILLEBEKE	December 27th		Company remained in trenches. Work continued as above. During the morning and afternoon there was H.T.M. activity on both sides especially in the ~~neighbourhood~~ of HEDGE STREET and SANCTUARY WOOD.	A.H.S.

2353 Wt. W2544/1454 700,000 5/15 D. D. & L. A.D.S.S./Forms/C. 2118.

Army Form C. 2118.

WAR DIARY
or
~~INTELLIGENCE SUMMARY.~~
(Erase heading not required.)

Instructions regarding War Diaries and Intelligence Summaries are contained in F. S. Regs., Part II. and the Staff Manual respectively. Title pages will be prepared in manuscript.

Place	Date	Hour	Summary of Events and Information	Remarks and references to Appendices
ZILLEBEKE	December 28th		Company remained in trenches. Work carried out as above. Enemy artillery activity above normal. TORR TOP, DAVISON STREET, MAPLE COPSE & SANCTUARY WOOD were heavily shelled at intervals during the day.	AHS.
ZILLEBEKE	December 29th		Company remained in trenches. Alternative emplacement constructed for ~~SOUTH~~ ^ABG^ STAFFORD STREET SOUTH. Enemy artillery & H.T.M. activity again above normal in this sector.	AHS.
ZILLEBEKE	December 30th		~~Intern~~ ^AHS^ Company remained in trenches. Intersection relief carried out. Work carried out as usual.	AHS.
ZILLEBEKE	December 31st		Company remained in trenches. Considerable artillery & H.T.M. activity on both sides throughout the day, especially between 2 pm and 4 pm.	AHS.
ZILLEBEKE	Jan 1st 1917		War Diary Completed for December 1916.	AHS.

[illegible signature] Capt
Commdg. 69th Coy. M.G.C.

2353 Wt. W2544/1454 700,000 5/15 D. D. & L. A.D.S.S./Forms/C. 2118.

Instructions regarding War Diaries and Intelligence Summaries are contained in F. S. Regs., Part II. and the Staff Manual respectively. Title pages will be prepared in manuscript.

WAR DIARY
or
~~INTELLIGENCE SUMMARY.~~
(Erase heading not required.)

Army Form C. 2118.

69 M G Coy
Vol 12

Place	Date	Hour	Summary of Events and Information	Remarks and references to Appendices
ZILLEBEKE	Jan: 1st 1917		Company remained in trenches. There was heavy shelling on both sides between 2 pm and 4 pm and between 5.20 pm & 6.20 pm. During this latter period the enemy violently bombarded our front line from SANCTUARY WOOD to HILL 60 using a considerable number of 5.9 and H.T.M.	AHG.
ZILLEBEKE	Jan 2nd		Company remained in trenches. Situation quiet. Extract from Supplement to London Gazette 2/1/17.	AHG.
			Captn W.M.H. Hungerford-Pollen — Military Cross.	
			Lieut J.W.H. Toynbee — Military Cross.	
			Lieut (T/Captn) H.G.V. Roberts — Mention.	
			Lieut C.F.T. Baker — Mention.	AHG.
ZILLEBEKE	Jan 3rd		Company remained in trenches. Situation quiet except during the afternoon when our artillery bombarded enemy front and support between MOUNT SORREL and HILL 60. Work continued on dugouts and emplacements.	AHG.
ZILLEBEKE	Jan 4th		Company remained in trenches. Situation quiet. Work continued	AHG.
ZILLEBEKE	Jan: 5th		Company remained in trenches. Reciprocal artillery & H.T.M. activity during the	

2353 Wt. W2544/1454 700,000 5/15 D. D. & L. A.D.S.S./Forms/C. 2118.

Army Form C. 2118.

Instructions regarding War Diaries and Intelligence Summaries are contained in F. S. Regs., Part II. and the Staff Manual respectively. Title pages will be prepared in manuscript.

WAR DIARY

or

~~INTELLIGENCE SUMMARY.~~

(Erase heading not required.)

Place	Date	Hour	Summary of Events and Information	Remarks and references to Appendices
ZILLEBEKE	Jan 5th		afternoon in the neighbourhood of MOUNT SORREL Work continued as usual.	AHS.
ZILLEBEKE	Jan 6th		Company remained in trenches Situation quiet. Work continued as usual	AHS.
ZILLEBEKE / ERIE CAMP.	Jan 7th		Company relieved by 70th M. G. C. Between 2 p.m. and 3 p.m. several H.S. were fired on the BUND. From 3.30 p.m. to 4.30 p.m. several hundred 4.2 and 5.9 fell in the vicinity of the BUND. A number of direct hits were obtained on the dugouts and several casualties resulted. Between 7 p.m. and 9 p.m. YPRES was heavily shelled with 5.9. Relief complete by 9.15 p.m. On relief company marched to huts in ERIE CAMP arriving about 12 M.N.	AHS.
ERIE CAMP.	Jan 8th		Company in huts at ERIE CAMP.	AHS.
ERIE CAMP	Jan 9th		Company in huts at ERIE CAMP. During morning and afternoon Company paraded for fatigues, gun cleaning ~~[illegible]~~ cleaning camp.	AHS
ERIE CAMP	Jan 10th		Company in huts at ERIE CAMP. Company employed on fatigues; one section on Revolver Practice. LIEUT H.J. DAWSON appointed 2nd in Command No 96 M.G. Coy.	AHS.
ERIE CAMP.	Jan 11th		Company in huts at ERIE CAMP. Company employed on fatigues; one section on Revolver Practice.	AHS.

2353 Wt. W2544/1454 700,000 5/15 D. D. & L. A.D.S.S./Forms/C. 2118.

Instructions regarding War Diaries and Intelligence Summaries are contained in F. S. Regs., Part II. and the Staff Manual respectively. Title pages will be prepared in manuscript.

WAR DIARY
or
~~INTELLIGENCE~~ SUMMARY.

(Erase heading not required.)

Army Form C. 2118.

Place	Date	Hour	Summary of Events and Information	Remarks and references to Appendices
ERIE CAMP	Jan 12th		Company in huts at ERIE CAMP. } Working parties found daily as	AHS.
ERIE CAMP	Jan 13th		Company in huts at ERIE CAMP } above. No training beyond Revolver practice	AHS.
ERIE CAMP	Jan 14th		Company in huts at ERIE CAMP } could be carried out.	AHS.
ERIE CAMP YPRES	Jan 15th		Company relieved 68th M.G.C. in the left sector of the Divisional Front. Relief Complete by 10.15 p.m. Dispositions as follows. (a) In the line 9 guns Right group: ZILLEBEKE, DORMY HOUSE, ROSLYN STREET, YEOMANRY POST (4 guns) under 2/Lt H WILSON at WELLINGTON CRESCENT. Left group: GORDON HOUSE, CHINA WALL, RITZ STREET (I17.c.4.9 – Reference ZILLEBEKE 1/10,000) LEINSTER STREET, FRONT LINE. (5 guns) under ~~2/Lt~~ Lt H.G.C. MEAD at HALF WAY HOUSE. (b) At the BUND (3 guns) under Sgt COUCHMAN. (c) IN YPRES – Company H.Q. (MAISON DE POZIERES) and 4 gun teams. One officer and 48 O.R. attached from 194 M.G. Coy for instruction and work on M.G. tunnels in RITZ STREET and WELLINGTON CRESCENT.	AHS.
YPRES	Jan 16th		Company remained in trenches. Working parties found during turn of duty for GORDON HOUSE (New position) ~~HALF~~ FRONT LINE (alternative emplacement)	

2353 Wt. W2544/1454 700,000 5/15 D. D. & L. A.D.S.S./Forms/C. 2118.

Army Form C. 2118.

Instructions regarding War Diaries and Intelligence Summaries are contained in F. S. Regs., Part II. and the Staff Manual respectively. Title pages will be prepared in manuscript.

WAR DIARY
or
INTELLIGENCE SUMMARY.

(*Erase heading not required.*)

Place	Date	Hour	Summary of Events and Information	Remarks and references to Appendices
			RITZ STREET (Tunnels and A.A. position) WELLINGTON CRESCENT (Tunnel) and ROSSLYN STREET (alternative emplacement). Situation normal.	AHG.
YPRES	Jan. 17th		Company remained in trenches. Situation normal.	AHG.
YPRES	Jan 18th		Company remained in trenches Situation normal.	AHG.
YPRES	Jan 19th		Company remained in trenches. Intersection relief of gun teams in the line carried out. Relief complete by 6 p.m.	AHG.
YPRES	Jan 20th		Company remained in trenches. Situation normal.	AHG.
YPRES	Jan 21st		Company remained in trenches. Situation normal.	AHG.
YPRES	Jan 22nd		Company remained in trenches. Situation normal.	AHG.
YPRES	Jan 23rd		Company remained in trenches. Intersection relief of gun teams in the line carried out. Situation normal	AHG.
YPRES	Jan 24th		Company remained in trenches. Owing to continuance of the frost, it was found impossible to continue work on concrete emplacements at GORDON HOUSE, ROSSLYN STREET and YETHANRY FORT. During the night 750 rounds were fired from ROSSLYN STREET on a gap in enemy wire at I 18 b 85.05 caused by our artillery. 500 rounds were also fired from	

2353 Wt. W2544/1454 700,000 5/15 D. D. & L. A.D.S.S./Forms/C. 2118.

Instructions regarding War Diaries and Intelligence Summaries are contained in F. S. Regs., Part II. and the Staff Manual respectively. Title pages will be prepared in manuscript.

WAR DIARY
or
~~INTELLIGENCE SUMMARY.~~
(Erase heading not required.)

Army Form C. 2118.

Place	Date	Hour	Summary of Events and Information	Remarks and references to Appendices
YPRES	24th Jan.		LEINSTER STREET on STIRLING CASTLE (J 13 d 50.38) Situation normal.	AHG.
			2/Lt A.S. DAVIDSON and 2/Lt D. ANDERSON reported for duty from BASE & were taken on the strength of the company accordingly	AHG
YPRES	25th Jan.		Company remained in trenches. During the day firing was carried out from an emplacement at I 16 d 95.97. 250 rounds were fired on HOOGE CHATEAU GROUNDS (I 18 b 70.80); 250 rounds were fired on SCREENS on the MENIN ROAD (J 13 b.70.80) and 500 rounds on TRENCH TRAMWAY JUNCTION W. of STIRLING CASTLE. During the night, 750 rounds were fired as on 24.1.17 on gap in hostile wire. Situation normal.	AHG.
YPRES	26th Jan.		Company remained in trenches. Situation normal.	[illegible]
YPRES	27th Jan.		Company remained in the line. Intermittent [illegible] without casualties. Situation normal.	[illegible]
YPRES	28th Jan.		Company remained in trenches. Our gun at ROSSLYN STREET fired 750 rounds at gap in enemy wire. Situation normal.	[illegible]

2353 Wt. W2544/1454 700,000 5/15 D. D. & L. A.D.S.S./Forms/C. 2118.

Army Form C. 2118.

Instructions regarding War Diaries and Intelligence Summaries are contained in F. S. Regs., Part II. and the Staff Manual respectively. Title pages will be prepared in manuscript.

WAR DIARY
or
~~INTELLIGENCE SUMMARY.~~
(Erase heading not required.)

Place	Date	~~Hour~~	Summary of Events and Information	Remarks and references to Appendices
YPRES.	Jan. 29th		Company remained in trenches. No firing by our guns. Situation normal.	MR
YPRES.	Jan. 30th		Company remained in trenches. Situation normal. G. H. Q. 2nd Line reconnoitred by Capt. FREEMAN and LIEUT. TOYNBEE.	MR
YPRES.	Jan. 31st		Situation remained ~~quiet~~ quiet. Company relieved in the line by 70 Company M. G. Corps. Relief complete by 10pm. Company marched to huts at ERIE CAMP (G 11 c 80.30).	MT.
ERIE CAMP	Feb. 1st		Company remained in ERIE CAMP. WAR DIARY completed for January 1917.	MR.
			[signature] Captain Commanding 69 Company M. G. Corps. 1/2/17.	

2353 Wt. W2544/1454 700,000 5/15 D. D. & L. A.D.S.S./Forms/C. 2118.

Instructions regarding War Diaries and Intelligence Summaries are contained in F. S. Regs., Part II. and the Staff Manual respectively. Title pages will be prepared in manuscript.

Army Form C. 2118.

WAR DIARY
or
~~INTELLIGENCE~~ SUMMARY.

(Erase heading not required.)

69 M G Coy
Vol 13

Place	Date	Hour	Summary of Events and Information	Remarks and references to Appendices
ERIE CAMP	1st Feb.		Company remained in huts at ERIE CAMP.	AHS.
ERIE CAMP	2nd Feb		Company remained in huts at ERIE CAMP. Fatigue party found for BUSSEBOOM.	AHS
ERIE CAMP	3rd Feb.		Company remained in huts at ERIE CAMP. Brigade billeting area visited by CORPS COMMANDER during the morning. Fatigue party found as above	AHS
ERIE CAMP	4th Feb.		Company remained in huts at ERIE CAMP. Parade Services in the morning. Fatigue party found as above.	AHS
ERIE CAMP	5th Feb.		Company remained in huts at ERIE CAMP. Section parades & fatigue. 2/Lt F. ENTWISLE [illegible] 4 U.K. & struck off the strength. Authority A.G. No. G. 4/6505K 25/4/17	AHS.
ERIE CAMP	6th Feb.		Company remained in huts at ERIE CAMP Section parades & fatigue.	AHS
ERIE CAMP	7th Feb		Company remained in huts at ERIE CAMP.	AHS
ERIE CAMP / ZILLEBEKE	8th Feb.		Company paraded for the trenches at 5.0 pm proceeding to YPRES by rail. Relief of 68th M.G.C. in the right section of the Divisional front complete by 9.55 pm. Disposition as follows: In the line 12 guns. 'A' Group 3 guns — RUDKIN HOUSE NORTH I24c.15.25, RUDKIN HOUSE SOUTH I24c 60.18, VALLEY COTTAGE, under Lt M.G.C. HEAD at RUDKIN HOUSE; 'B' Group 4 guns at OBSERVATORY HOLE I 24 c 59.25, DUMP HOLE I 24 c 70.30, HALIFAX STREET I 24 c 70.25, STAFFORD ST NORTH I 24 c 35.70. under 2/Lt D. ANDERSON at PETROGRAD sup.	AHS.

2353 Wt. W2544/1454 700,000 5/15 D. D. & L. A.D.S.S./Forms/C. 2118.

Instructions regarding War Diaries and Intelligence Summaries are contained in F. S. Regs., Part II. and the Staff Manual respectively. Title pages will be prepared in manuscript.

WAR DIARY
or
INTELLIGENCE SUMMARY.
(Erase heading not required.)

Army Form C. 2118.

Place	Date	Hour	Summary of Events and Information	Remarks and references to Appendices
ZILLEBEKE.	8th Feb.		"C" Group 3 guns at HEDGE STREET I 30 b.12.62, REDAN I 24 d 25.35 and SPY HOLE I 24 c 93,21 under Lt C.W. SYMES in PETROGRAD SAP; and "D" Group 2 guns at METROPOLITAN TRENCH I 29 c 70.95 and SCHOOL HOUSE I 22 d 90.65 under 2/Lt A.S. DAVIDSON. at ZILLEBEKE. Company Headquarters at the BUND with 1 section complete. Working parties found during tour of duty for HEDGE STREET, N.W. Corner of BUND (concrete emplacement)	A.H.G.
ZILLEBEKE	9th Feb.		Company remained in trenches. Situation quiet } Owing to severe frost very little	A.H.G.
ZILLEBEKE	10th Feb.		Company remained in trenches. Situation Quiet. } work could be carried out	A.H.G.
ZILLEBEKE	11th Feb.		Company remained in trenches Situation Quiet }	A.H.G.
ZILLEBEKE	12th Feb.		Company remained in trenches. Situation quiet. Interaction relief of teams in the line.	A.H.G.
ZILLEBEKE	13th Feb.		Company remained in trenches Situation quiet. Work continued on N.W. Corner of BUND	A.H.G.
ZILLEBEKE	14th Feb.		Company remained in trenches. Situation quiet Work continued as above	A.H.G.
ZILLEBEKE	15th Feb.		Company remained in trenches. Situation quiet. 1 O.R. wounded. Work continued as above. New dugout commenced in tunnel for HALIFAX HOLE.	A.H.G.
ZILLEBEKE	16th Feb.		Company remained in trenches. Situation quiet. Work continued. Intersection	

Army Form C. 2118.

Instructions regarding War Diaries and Intelligence Summaries are contained in F. S. Regs., Part II. and the Staff Manual respectively. Title pages will be prepared in manuscript.

WAR DIARY
or
INTELLIGENCE SUMMARY.

(Erase heading not required.)

Place	Date	Hour	Summary of Events and Information	Remarks and references to Appendices
ZILLEBEKE	16th Feb		relief of gun teams in the line complete by 7 pm.	AHG.
ZILLEBEKE	17th Feb		Company remained in trenches. During the night there was an enemy raid N. North of the MENIN ROAD and considerable artillery activity on both sides	AHG
ZILLEBEKE	18th Feb.		Company remained in trenches. At 8 pm. a small raid was carried out South of SANCTUARY WOOD. Situation quiet by 10 pm.	AHG.
ZILLEBEKE	19th Feb.		Company remained in trenches. Situation quiet	AHG
ZILLEBEKE	20th Feb.		Company remained in trenches. At 3 am. a raid was carried out N. of MOUNT SORREL. Hostile artillery retaliated on our front & support lines. Guns at REDAN and SPY HOLE were hit by shrapnel but no damage was done. Situation was quiet by 4.30 am. At 5 pm an extensive raid was carried out S of HILL 60 and a bluff raid was carried out on HILL 60, two small mines being sprung. Enemy retaliated heavily on the Brigade front for 1½ hours. Situation was quiet by 7.30 pm. Intersection relief of gun teams	
~~ZILLEBEKE~~				AHG.
ZILLEBEKE	21st Feb.		Company remained in trenches. Situation quiet. in the line complete by 4 pm.	AHG.
ZILLEBEKE	22nd Feb.		Company remained in trenches. Situation quiet	AHG.
ZILLEBEKE	23rd Feb.		Company remained in trenches. Situation quiet. 500 rounds fired during the	

2353 Wt. W2544/1454 700,000 5/15 D. D. & L. A.D.S.S./Forms/C. 2118.

Army Form C. 2118.

Instructions regarding War Diaries and Intelligence Summaries are contained in F. S. Regs., Part II. and the Staff Manual respectively. Title pages will be prepared in manuscript.

WAR DIARY
or
~~INTELLIGENCE SUMMARY.~~
(Erase heading not required.)

Place	Date	Hour	Summary of Events and Information	Remarks and references to Appendices
ZILLEBEKE	23rd Feb		afternoon on Support line & Trench Tramway S. of KLEIN ZILLEBEKE. 7 O.R. reported as reinforcements from M. G. Base Depot. Situation quiet. Work continued as above	AHG.
ZILLEBEKE	24th Feb.		Company remained in trenches. Situation quiet. Work continued as above	AHG.
ZILLEBEKE	25th Feb		Company relieved by 116th M.G. Coy. Relief complete by 12.50 am 26.2.17. On relief Company marched to huts at ERIE CAMP.	AHG.
ERIE CAMP.	26th Feb.		Company remained in huts at ERIE CAMP	AHG.
ERIE CAMP.) HERZEELE (	27th Feb.		Company paraded at 9.15 am and marched by road with 69th Infantry Brigade to billets in HERZEELE arriving at about 4 pm.	AHG.
HERZEELE) MERCKEGHEM (	28th Feb.		Company paraded at 10.0 am and marched by road with 69th Infantry Brigade to billets in MERCKEGHEM, arriving at about 3.45 pm	AHG.
MERCKEGHEM BAYENGHEM LES-EPERLEQUES	1st March		Company paraded 9.30 am & marched by road with 69th Infantry ~~Bri~~ Brigade to billets in BAYENGHEM-LES-EPERLEQUES arriving at about 3.30 pm. War Diary Complete for February 1917	AHG.

[signature] Captain
Commanding 69th Coy. Machine Gun Corps

2353 Wt. W2544/1454 700,000 5/15 D. D. & L. A.D.S.S./Forms/C. 2118.

Instructions regarding War Diaries and Intelligence Summaries are contained in F. S. Regs., Part II. and the Staff Manual respectively. Title pages will be prepared in manuscript.

WAR DIARY

~~or~~

~~INTELLIGENCE SUMMARY.~~

(Erase heading not required.)

Army Form C. 2118.

69 M G Coy
Vol 14

Place	Date	Hour	Summary of Events and Information	Remarks and references to Appendices
MERKEGHEM to BAYENGHEM LEZ EPERLEQUES	1st		Company paraded at 9.30 am outside billets in MERKEGHEM and marched by road into 69th Infantry Brigade billets in BAYENGHEM-LEZ-EPERLEQUES arriving at about 3.30 p.m.	AHS
BAYENGHEM.	2nd		Company remained in billets at BAYENGHEM-LEZ-EPERLEQUES. Company and recreational training	AHS.
BAYENGHEM	3rd		Company remained in billets at BAYENGHEM-LEZ-EPERLEQUES. Company and recreational training	AHS
BAYENGHEM	4th		Company remained in billets at BAYENGHEM-LEZ-EPERLEQUES. Company and recreational training. 5569 Sgt W. Cochrane proceeded 10th G.C. Base Depot. Authority A.G's No. 6864 dated 23.10.16.	AHS.
BAYENGHEM	5th		Company remained in billets at BAYENGHEM-LEZ-EPERLEQUES. Company & recreational training	AHS
BAYENGHEM	6th		Company remained in billets at BAYENGHEM-LEZ-EPERLEQUES. Company and recreational training. Three sections fired on 30x range at G.2.c.4.7.	AHS
BAYENGHEM.	7th		Company remains in billets at BAYENGHEM-LEZ-EPERLEQUES. 9 am to 1 pm. Tactical exercise on training area. One section at Brigade Bombing School at EPERLEQUES.	

2353 Wt. W2544/1454 700,000 5/15 D. D. & L. A.D.S.S./Forms/C. 2118.

Instructions regarding War Diaries and Intelligence Summaries are contained in F. S. Regs., Part II. and the Staff Manual respectively. Title pages will be prepared in manuscript.

WAR DIARY

or

~~INTELLIGENCE SUMMARY~~.

(*Erase heading not required.*)

Army Form C. 2118.

Place	Date	Hour	Summary of Events and Information	Remarks and references to Appendices
BAYENGHEM.	8th		Company remained in billets at BAYENGHEM-LEZ-EPERLEQUES 9.0 am. to 1 pm. [illegible] one Section fired on 30 yds range at Q 2 c 4.7, one section at Brigade Bombing School at EPERLEQUES two sections Tactical exercise on Training area. 2 pm to 4 pm – Recreational training.	AHG
BAYENGHEM	9th		Company remained in billets at BAYENGHEM-LEZ-EPERLEQUES. 9.0 am to 1 pm. Section training – One section at Brigade Bombing School EPERLEQUES. 1 O.R. reported for duty from M.G. Base Depot. 2 pm. to 4 pm. Recreational Training	AHG
BAYENGHEM	10th		Company remained in billets at BAYENGHEM-LEZ-EPERLEQUES. 9 am. to 1 pm. Tactical exercise on Training area – 2 pm to 4 pm. one Section at Brigade Bombing School, EPERLEQUES.	AHG
BAYENGHEM	11th		Company remained in billets at BAYENGHEM-LEZ-EPERLEQUES. Company & recreational training	AHG
BAYENGHEM	12th		Company remained in billets at BAYENGHEM-LEZ-EPERLEQUES 9 am to 1 pm. Tactical Exercise on Training area	AHG
BAYENGHEM	13th		Company remained in billets at BAYENGHEM-LEZ-EPERLEQUES. 8 am. to 11 am. Baths at HOULE 11 am. to 1 pm. Section Training 2 pm to 4 pm. Recreational Training	AHG

2353 Wt. W2544/1454 700,000 5/15 D. D. & L. A.D.S.S./Forms/C. 2118.

Instructions regarding War Diaries and Intelligence Summaries are contained in F. S. Regs., Part II. and the Staff Manual respectively. Title pages will be prepared in manuscript.

WAR DIARY
or
INTELLIGENCE SUMMARY.
(Erase heading not required.)

Army Form C. 2118.

Place	Date	Hour	Summary of Events and Information	Remarks and references to Appendices
BAYENGHEM	14th		Company remained in billets at BAYENGHEM LEZ - EPERLEQUES. 7.30 am to 11.30 am. One section on 30x Range at Q 2 c 4.7. Three sections: Tactical exercises on Training Area 11.30 am 1.30 pm. Gas Test at EPERLEQUES	AHP.
BAYENGHEM	15th		Company remained in billets at BAYENGHEM - LEZ - EPERLEQUES 9.30 am to 4.30 pm Brigade exercise on Training Area	AHP.
BAYENGHEM	16th		Company remained in billets at BAYENGHEM - LEZ - EPERLEQUES. 9 am to 1 pm One section on 30x range at Q 2. c. 4.7, Two sections Section Training. One section at Brigade BOMBING School EPERLEQUES.	AHP.
BAYENGHEM	17th		Company remained in billets at BAYENGHEM - LEZ - EPERLEQUES 9 am to 1 pm One section on 30x range at Q 2 c. 4.7. Two sections Section Training. One section at Brigade Bombing School EPERLEQUES. 2 pm to 4 pm Recreational Training 1. OR reported for duty from M. G. Base Depot	AHP.
BAYENGHEM	18th		Company remained in billets at BAYENGHEM - LEZ - EPERLEQUES. 10 am Inspection by OC. Coy 10.45 am Parade Service 11.0 am.	AHP.
BAYENGHEM. MERKEGHEM	19th		Company parade 8 am outside billets and marched with 69th Infantry Brigade	

2353 Wt. W2544/1454 700,000 5/15 D. D. & L. A.D.S.S./Forms/C. 2118.

Army Form C. 2118.

WAR DIARY

or

~~INTELLIGENCE SUMMARY.~~

(Erase heading not required.)

Instructions regarding War Diaries and Intelligence Summaries are contained in F. S. Regs., Part II. and the Staff Manual respectively. Title pages will be prepared in manuscript.

Place	Date	Hour	Summary of Events and Information	Remarks and references to Appendices
BAYENGHEM	19th March		to billets in MERKEGHEM arriving at about 12 noon.	A.H.S.
MERKEGHEM				
MERKEGHEM	20th		Company paraded outside billets at 8.30 am and marched with 69th Infantry	
HOUTKERQUE			Brigade to billets in HOUTKERQUE, arriving at 1.50 pm	A.H.S.
HOUTKERQUE	21st		Company paraded outside billets at 9 am and marched with 69th Infantry Brigade	
"Y" CAMP.			to billets in "Y" CAMP on HOUTKERQUE-POPERINGHE road, arriving at 11.45 am.	A.H.S.
"Y" CAMP	22nd		Company in huts at "Y" CAMP	A.H.S.
"Y" CAMP	23rd		Company in huts at "Y" CAMP. Extract from LONDON GAZETTE dated March 20th	A.H.S.
~~"Y" CAMP 24th~~			1917 "The undermentioned to be Temporary Lieutenants	
			Temp 2nd Lieut C. Lindsay . Dated Jany 1st 1917	A.H.S.
"Y" CAMP	24th		Company in huts at "Y" CAMP }	A.H.S.
"Y" CAMP	25th		Company in huts at "Y" CAMP } Company and recreational training	A.H.S.
"Y" CAMP	26th		Company in huts at "Y" CAMP } at "Y" CAMP.	A.H.S.
"Y" CAMP	27th		Company in huts at "Y" CAMP.	A.H.S.
"Y" CAMP	28th		Company in huts at "Y" CAMP } Inspection by ARMY COMMANDER at 2 pm	A.H.S.
"Y" CAMP	29th		Company in huts at "Y" CAMP }	A.H.S.

2353 Wt. W2544/1454 700,000 5/15 D. D. & L. A.D.S.S./Forms/C. 2118.

Instructions regarding War Diaries and Intelligence Summaries are contained in F. S. Regs., Part II. and the Staff Manual respectively. Title pages will be prepared in manuscript.

WAR DIARY

~~or~~

~~INTELLIGENCE SUMMARY.~~

(Erase heading not required.)

Army Form C. 2118.

Place	Date	Hour	Summary of Events and Information	Remarks and references to Appendices
"Y" CAMP	30th March		Company in huts at "Y" CAMP } Company & recreational training in "Y" CAMP.	AHG.
"Y" CAMP	31st March		Company in huts at "Y" CAMP. }	AHG.
"Y" CAMP	1st April		Company in huts at "Y" CAMP. }	
			War Diary Completed for March 1917.	AHG.

No. 69 MACHINE GUN COMPANY.
No. ....
Date 2-4-17

[signature] Capt.
COMDG. No. 69 M. G. COY.

To.
Staff Captain,
69th. Infantry Brigade.
- - - - - - - - - - - - - - - - -

Attached please find War Diary for the month of April 1917.

[signature] Captain.
Commanding 69th. Company Machine Gun Corps.

No. 69
MACHINE GUN
COMPANY.
No. BY/91
Date 3-5-17

Instructions regarding War Diaries and Intelligence Summaries are contained in F. S. Regs., Part II. and the Staff Manual respectively. Title pages will be prepared in manuscript.

WAR DIARY
or
~~INTELLIGENCE SUMMARY.~~
(Erase heading not required.)

Army Form C. 2118.

69 M G Coy
Vol 15

Place	Date	Hour	Summary of Events and Information	Remarks and references to Appendices
"Y" CAMP.	April 1st		Company in huts at "Y" CAMP	AHS.
"Y" CAMP	April 2nd		Company in huts at "Y" CAMP	AHS.
"Y" CAMP	April 3rd		Company in huts at "Y" CAMP.	AHS.
"Y" CAMP	April 4th		Company in huts at "Y" CAMP. Inspection by G.O.C. 69th Infantry Brigade at 10.0 am. Intersection Competition for Turn-out, Transport and Action from Limbers	AHS.
"Y" CAMP	April 5th		Company in huts at "Y" CAMP.	AHS.
Y CAMP / TORONTO	April 6th		Company moves to TORONTO CAMP arriving at about 6.30 pm.	AHS.
TORONTO CAMP	April 7th		Company in huts at TORONTO CAMP. [struck out] AHS.	AHS.
TORONTO CAMP	April 8th		Company in huts at TORONTO CAMP. CHURCH PARADE 12 NOON.	AHS.
TORONTO CAMP	April 9th		Company in huts at TORONTO CAMP. 9 am to 12 noon SECTION TRAINING	AHS.
TORONTO CAMP	April 10th		Company in huts at TORONTO CAMP. 9 am to 12 noon SECTION TRAINING.	AHS
TORONTO CAMP	April 11th		Company in huts at TORONTO CAMP 9 am to 12 noon SECTION TRAINING	AHS.

2353 Wt. W2544/1454 700,000 5/15 D. D. & L. A.D.S.S./Forms/C. 2118.

Army Form C. 2118.

WAR DIARY
or
INTELLIGENCE ~~SUMMARY~~.
(*Erase heading not required.*)

Instructions regarding War Diaries and Intelligence Summaries are contained in F. S. Regs., Part II. and the Staff Manual respectively. Title pages will be prepared in manuscript.

Place	Date	Hour	Summary of Events and Information	Remarks and references to Appendices
TORONTO CAMP / WINNIPEG	April 12th		Company moved to WINNIPEG CAMP arriving at 2.30 pm. 3. OR reported as re-inforcements from BASE DEPOT.	AHG
WINNIPEG CAMP	April 13th		Company in huts at WINNIPEG CAMP 9. am to 12 NOON SECTION TRAINING.	AHG
" CAMP	April 14th		Company in huts at WINNIPEG CAMP 9 am to 12 NOON SECTION TRAINING, Company paraded for baths at 1.45 pm.	AHG
" CAMP / HILL 60	April 15th		Company in huts at WINNIPEG CAMP. Relief of 70th M. G. C. in the [illegible] right sector of the Divisional front, complete by 12 MN. Dispositions as follows Coy HQ and 2 guns in reserve RAILWAY DUGOUTS I 21 c. 35. 80 (Reference ZILLEBEKE SHEET 1/10,000) Right group two guns at [illegible] (I 28 d 54. 49) and C.6 (I 34 b 2.3) under Lt H. G. C. Mead at I 28 c. 90. 20. Centre group four guns at DUMP RIGHT (I 29 c. 2.4) DUMP LEFT (I 29 c. 25. 35) INFANTRY TUNNEL (I 29 c 10. 40) & LARCH WOOD (I 29 c 16. 89) under Lt G. W. SYMES at the DUMP. (I 29 c. 2. 4) Left group three guns at FOSSEWAY (I 23 a 20. 05) KNOLL FARM. (I 29 a 70. 72) and METROPOLITAN LEFT (I 29 a 70. 20) under Lt AH Graves at FOSSEWAY	

Instructions regarding War Diaries and Intelligence Summaries are contained in F. S. Regs., Part II. and the Staff Manual respectively. Title pages will be prepared in manuscript.

WAR DIARY

or

~~INTELLIGENCE~~ SUMMARY.

(Erase heading not required.)

Army Form C. 2118.

Place	Date	Hour	Summary of Events and Information	Remarks and references to Appendices
HILL 60	22nd April		Company remained in trenches (7500 rounds) Indirect fire carried out during the night on Dump at KLEIN ZILLEBEKE, the road between KLEIN ZILLEBEKE and ZANDVOORDE and a trench tramway in the neighbourhood.	AHG
HILL 60	23rd April		Two Sections of the Company relieved by two Sections 70th M.G.C. On relief these sections marched to huts at ERIE CAMP ~~[illegible]~~ arriving about 4 am 24-4-17 (7000 rounds) Indirect fire carried out on same area as previous night	AHG
HILL 60	24th April		Coy HQ and two SECTIONS remained in trenches. The two sections relieved on 23 4 17 marched to ABEELE and relieved two SECTIONS 70th M.G.C. on anti aircraft duty. Relief Complete by 5 pm. Indirect fire (6500 rounds) carried out on same area as previous night	AHG
HILL 60	28th April		Coy HQ and two SECTIONS ~~remained in trenches~~ relieved by Coy HQ and two SECTIONS 70th M.G.C. Relief Complete by 12 MN. On relief the Company marched to huts in ERIE CAMP.	AHG
HILL 60	26th April		Company in huts at ERIE CAMP	AHG

2353 Wt. W2544/1454 700,000 5/15 D. D. & L. A.D.S.S./Forms/C. 2118.

Instructions regarding War Diaries and Intelligence Summaries are contained in F. S. Regs., Part II. and the Staff Manual respectively. Title pages will be prepared in manuscript.

WAR DIARY
or
~~INTELLIGENCE SUMMARY.~~
(Erase heading not required.)

Army Form C. 2118.

69 M G Coy
Vol 16

Place	Date	Hour	Summary of Events and Information	Remarks and references to Appendices
STEENVOORDE	May 1st		Coy HQ and two Sections ~~[illegible]~~ in Billets (1½ mile N.W. of STEENVOORDE). 9.0 am to 12 NOON Section training. Two Sections at ABEELE	AttG.
STEENVOORDE	May 2nd		Coy H.Q. and two Sections in Billets (1½ miles N.W. of STEENVOORDE) Inspection ~~of Coy~~ by G.O.C. 23rd Division at 11.30 am. Two sections at ABEELE.	AttG.
STEENVOORDE	May 3rd		Coy HQ. and two Sections in Billets (1½ miles N.W. of STEENVOORDE) 9.0 am to 12 NOON Section training. Two Sections at ABEELE.	AttG.
STEENVOORDE	May 4th		Coy HQ. and two Section in Billets (1½ mile N.W. of STEENVOORDE.) 9.0 am. to 12 NOON Section training Two sections at ABEELE.	AttG.
STEENVOORDE	May 5th		Coy HQ. and two sections in Billets (1½ miles N.W. of STEENVOORDE), 9.0 am to 12 NOON Section training. Relief of two sections at ABEELE by two Sections at STEENVOORDE complete by 6 pm.	AttG.
STEENVOORDE	May 6th		Coy H.Q. and two sections in Billets (1½ mile N.W. of STEENVOORDE). Divine Service 11 am. Two Sections at ABEELE	AttG.
STEENVOORDE	May 7th		Coy HQ and two Section in Billets (1½ miles N.W. of STEENVOORDE) 9.30 am to 12.30 pm Tactical exercise in training area. Two Sections at ABEELE	AttG.
STEENVOORDE	May 8th		Coy H.Q. and two Sections in Billets (1½ miles N.W. of STEENVOORDE)	

Instructions regarding War Diaries and Intelligence Summaries are contained in F. S. Regs., Part II. and the Staff Manual respectively. Title pages will be prepared in manuscript.

WAR DIARY
or
~~INTELLIGENCE SUMMARY.~~
(Erase heading not required.)

Army Form C. 2118.

Place	Date	Hour	Summary of Events and Information	Remarks and references to Appendices
STEENVOORDE	May 8th (contd)		Section Training from 9.0 am. to 12 NOON. Two Sections at ABEELE	AHG.
STEENVOORDE	May 9th		Coy HQ and two Sections in billets (1½ miles N.W. of STEENVOORDE) 9.30 am to 12.30 pm Tactical exercise. Two sections at ABEELE.	AHG.
STEENVOORDE WINNIPEG CAMP	May 10th		Two sections at ABEELE relieved by two Sections from STEENVOORDE. On completion of relief at 4.0 pm two Sections & Coy HQ marched with 70th Infantry Brigade to huts in WINNIPEG CAMP, arriving at 7.15 pm.	AHG.
WINNIPEG CAMP	May 11th		~~[illegible]~~ Coy H.Q. and two sections at WINNIPEG CAMP. Two Sections at ABEELE. 4 OR reported from M. G. Base Depot for duty and taken on strength accordingly	AHG.
WINNIPEG CAMP	May 12th		Coy HQ and two Sections in huts at WINNIPEG CAMP. 9.0 am to 12.30 pm Section training. Two Sections at ABEELE.	AHG.
WINNIPEG CAMP	May 13th		Coy HQ and two sections in huts at WINNIPEG CAMP. Divine Service at 11.30 am. Two sections at ABEELE.	AHG.
WINNIPEG CAMP	May 14th		Coy HQ and two Sections in huts at WINNIPEG CAMP, 9.0 am to 12.30 pm Section training. Two sections at ABEELE.	AHG.
WINNIPEG CAMP	May 15th		Coy HQ and two sections in huts at WINNIPEG CAMP.	

2353 Wt. W2544/1454 700,000 5/15 D. D. & L. A.D.S.S./Forms/C. 2118.

Army Form C. 2118.

Instructions regarding War Diaries and Intelligence Summaries are contained in F. S. Regs., Part II. and the Staff Manual respectively. Title pages will be prepared in manuscript.

WAR DIARY
or
INTELLIGENCE SUMMARY.
(Erase heading not required.)

Place	Date	Hour	Summary of Events and Information	Remarks and references to Appendices
WINNIPEG Hu CAMP	May 16th		Company Headquarters and two sections in huts at WINNIPEG CAMP Two SECTIONS at ABEELE	AHG
WINNIPEG CAMP	May 17th		Company Headquarters and two Sections in huts at WINNIPEG CAMP Two Section at ABEELE	AHG
WINNIPEG CAMP	May 18th		Company Headquarters and two SECTIONS at WINNIPEG CAMP, Two Section at ABEELE	
HILL 60			Company Headquarters and two SECTIONS relieved Coy HQ and two SECTIONS 70th M.G.C. in the right sector of the Divisional Front. Relief Complete by 3 am Disposition as follows. Company Headquarters in RAILWAY DUGOUTS I 21.c 38.80 (Reference Map ZILLEBEKE SHEET 1/10,000) Four guns under Lt A.H. GRAVES M.C. at DUMP RIGHT (I29c 20.40), DUMP LEFT (I29c 25.35) INFANTRY TUNNEL (I29c 60.40) and LARCH WOOD (I29c 16.89) - Headquarters at the DUMP (I29c 20.40). Two guns under 2Lt D. ANDERSON at KNOLL FARM (I29a 70.72) and METROPOLITAN LEFT (I29a 70.20) - Headquarters MANOR FARM (I22c 70.50) Two guns under Lt H.G.C. MEAD at VERBRANDENMOLEN ROAD (I28a 24.83) and C 6. (I34b. 70.80) Headquarters I28.c 90.20	AHG
HILL 60	May 19th		Company Headquarters and two SECTIONS remained in trenches. Six guns	

2353 Wt. W2544/1454 700,000 5/15 D. D. & L. A.D.S.S./Forms/C. 2118.

Instructions regarding War Diaries and Intelligence Summaries are contained in F. S. Regs., Part II. and the Staff Manual respectively. Title pages will be prepared in manuscript.

WAR DIARY
or
~~INTELLIGENCE SUMMARY~~.

(Erase heading not required.)

Army Form C. 2118.

Place	Date	Hour	Summary of Events and Information	Remarks and references to Appendices
			Two Sections less one subsection	
HILL 60.	May 19th		at ABEELE relieved by six LEWIS GUNS X CORPS CYCLIST BATTALION. On relief Sections ~~marched to~~ relieved two Sections (less one subsection) 68th M.G.C. in the line. Relief complete by 2.0 am 20.5.17. One subsection remained at ABEELE	AHP
HILL 60	May 20th		The Company (less one subsection at ABEELE) remained in trenches. 5000 rounds indirect fire carried out during the night on hostile trench tramways and trench junctions.	AHP
HILL 60	May 21st		Company (less one subsection at ABEELE) remained in trenches. Indirect night firing carried out as above.	AHP
HILL 60	May 22nd		Company (less one subsection at ABEELE) remained in trenches. Subsection at ABEELE relieved by two guns 2nd CORPS CAVALRY. On relief subsection marched from ABEELE and relieved my subsection 68th M.G.C. in reserve at RAILWAY DUGOUTS. ~~Indirect~~ Relief complete by 12 M.N. Indirect night firing carried out as above	AHP
HILL 60	May 23rd		Company remained in trenches. Indirect night firing carried out as above.	AHP

2353 Wt. W2544/1454 700,000 5/15 D. D. & L. A.D.S.S./Forms/C. 2118.

WAR DIARY

or

INTELLIGENCE SUMMARY.

(Erase heading not required.)

Army Form C. 2118.

Instructions regarding War Diaries and Intelligence Summaries are contained in F. S. Regs., Part II. and the Staff Manual respectively. Title pages will be prepared in manuscript.

Place	Date	Hour	Summary of Events and Information	Remarks and references to Appendices
HILL 60 - BOESCHEPE	May 24th		Company relieved by 70th M. G. C. Relief complete by 3 0 am 25/5/17 On relief Company marched by sections to RAILWAY SIDING at BRANDHOEK and entrained for ABEELE. On arrival at ABEELE Company marched to billets near BOESCHEPE (R4 d) arriving at 7.15 am 25/5/17	AHG
BOESCHEPE	May 25th		Company remained in billets (Reference Sheet 27 d N.E.)	AHG
BOESCHEPE	May 26th		Company remained in billets. 2nd Lieut G SAXBY, 2nd Lieut W. R. HOLLOWAY reported for duty with Company from M. G BASE DEPOT and taken on the strength of the Company accordingly. Coy moved to new billets at R 3 a	AHG AHG
BOESCHEPE	May 27th		Company remained in billets	AHG
BOESCHEPE	May 28th		Company remained in billets. Company marched to practise trenches at R22, R27 and R28 and carried out tactical exercise during the morning. 2nd Lt R. FOORD KELCEY reported for duty with Company from M. G. BASE DEPOT and taken on the strength of the Company accordingly	AHG AHG
BOESCHEPE	May 29th		Company remained in billets. Company marched to practise trenches at R22, R27 and R28 and took part in Brigade Exercise during the morning	AHG
BOESCHEPE	May 30th		Company remained in billets Company marched to practise trenches and took	

2353 Wt. W2544/1454 700,000 5/15 D. D. & L. A.D.S.S./Forms/C. 2118.

Army Form C. 2118.

WAR DIARY

or

~~INTELLIGENCE~~ SUMMARY.

(*Erase heading not required.*)

Instructions regarding War Diaries and Intelligence Summaries are contained in F. S. Regs., Part II. and the Staff Manual respectively. Title pages will be prepared in manuscript.

Place	Date	Hour	Summary of Events and Information	Remarks and references to Appendices
BOESCHEPE	May 30th		in Brigade Exercise during the morning.	A.H.G.
BOESCHEPE	May 31st		[illegible, struck out]. Company paraded at 8 am and marched to camp at R5 Central arriving about 9 a.m.	A.H.G.
BOESCHEPE	June 1st		Company remained in camp at R5 central. WAR DIARY COMPLETED to 31 May 1917	A.H.G.

[signature] Capt

Comdg 69th Coy. M.G.C

2353 Wt. W2544/1454 700,000 5/15 D. D. & L. A.D.S.S./Forms/C. 2118.

Army Form C. 2118.

69 M G Coy

Vol 17

WAR DIARY
or
INTELLIGENCE ~~SUMMARY~~.

(Erase heading not required.)

Instructions regarding War Diaries and Intelligence Summaries are contained in F. S. Regs., Part II. and the Staff Manual respectively. Title pages will be prepared in manuscript.

Place	Date	Hour	Summary of Events and Information	Remarks and references to Appendices
BOESCHEPE	1st June 1917		Company remained in camp at R.S. central. Extract from LONDON GAZETTE dated 15.5.17. MENTIONED IN DESPATCHES. 5586 C.S.M. WOOLMER. R. 6570 Sgt DAVISON. J.	AHJ
BOESCHEPE	2nd June		Company remained in camp at R.S. central (Reference Map Sheet 27 D.S.E)	
BOESCHEPE / OUDERDOM	3rd June		Company paraded 6 pm and marched to BIVOUACKS at G18c. 90.60 (Reference Map Sheet 28 N.W.) arriving about 7.30 pm	AHJ
OUDERDOM.	4th June.		Coy H.Q. and two Sections remained in BIVOUACKS at G18c 90.60 (1500x N.W. of OUDERDOM) ~~[illegible]~~ 4 guns relieved 8 guns 68 M.G.C. in the line in the HILL 60 SUBSECTOR. ~~[illegible]~~ 4 guns moved into COPPICE on S. Bank of ZILLEBEKE LAKE	AHJ
OUDERDOM / HILL 60.	5th June		Coy H.Q. and two Sections moved into COPPICE on S. Bank of ZILLEBEKE LAKE, arriving about 12 M.N. Two Sections remained in trenches	AHJ
HILL 60.	6th June.		Company - less ~~[illegible]~~ 4 guns - remained in COPPICE on S. Bank of ZILLEBEKE LAKE ~~[illegible]~~ Two guns remained at INFANTRY TUNNEL + LARCH WOOD under 2/Lt L.R. HOLLOWAY	

2353 Wt. W2544/1454 700,000 5/15 D. D. & L. A.D.S.S./Forms/C. 2118.

Army Form C. 2118.

WAR DIARY

or

~~INTELLIGENCE SUMMARY~~

(Erase heading not required.)

Instructions regarding War Diaries and Intelligence Summaries are contained in F. S. Regs., Part II. and the Staff Manual respectively. Title pages will be prepared in manuscript.

Place	Date	Hour	Summary of Events and Information	Remarks and references to Appendices
HILL 60.	6th Jun		at INFANTRY TUNNEL. Two guns at C6 and L10 under 2/Lt D. ANDERSON at C6. One O.R. wounded. At 10 pm. 6 gun teams moved into their assembly positions all teams being in position by 12 M.N.	AHF
II				AHF
HILL 60	7th Jun		Company remained in trenches. OPERATION ORDERS for the attack, and a detailed report of the attack on HILL 60 and subsequent operations during this period are attached in APPENDICES "A" & "B". Details of casualties are shewn in APPENDIX "C".	
HILL 60	8th Jun			
HILL 60	9th Jun			
HILL 60	10th Jun			
HILL 60	11th Jun			AHF
HILL 60	12th Jun		Company relieved by 17th M.G.C. Owing to shelling & other causes the relief was not complete till 3.0 am 13.6.17.	
VANCOUVER CAMP.				AHF
VANCOUVER CAMP.	13th Jun		On completion of relief the company proceeded by MOTOR LORRY & MOTOR OMNIBUS to huts at VANCOUVER CAMP, sections arriving in the order of their relief. Coy H.Q. arrived at about 7.0 am. Company paraded at 6 pm. &	
ROUCHLOCHE				

Instructions regarding War Diaries and Intelligence Summaries are contained in F. S. Regs., Part II. and the Staff Manual respectively. Title pages will be prepared in manuscript.

WAR DIARY
or
~~INTELLIGENCE SUMMARY.~~

(Erase heading not required.)

Army Form C. 2118.

Place	Date	Hour	Summary of Events and Information	Remarks and references to Appendices
			Marched by road with 69th Infantry Brigade to billets at R32 d 70.20 (Reference Map Sheet 27) arriving at about 10.30 pm.	AHG
ROUKLOSHILLE	14th June		Company remained in billets at R32 d 70.20. 4 OR reported as reinforcements from M. G. Base Dept.	AHG
ROUKLOSHILLE	15th June		Company remained in billets	AHG
ROUKLOSHILLE	16th June		Company remained in billets. Inspection by DIVISIONAL COMMANDER at 10.30 am. 15 OR reported as reinforcements from M. G. Base Dept.	AHG
ROUKLOSHILLE	17th June		Company remained in billets.	AHG
ROUKLOSHILLE	18th June		Company remained in billets	AHG
ROUKLOSHILLE	19th June		Company remained in billets. Brigade Horse and Transport Competition 1st Prize for Mess Cart & 3rd Prize in MULE RACE won by Company. 20 OR reported as reinforcement from M. G. Base Dept.	AHG
ROUKLOSHILLE	20th June		Company remained in billets. } Work confined to section training, & short route marches	AHG
ROUKLOSHILLE	21st June		Company remained in billets }	AHG
ROUKLOSHILLE	22nd June		Company remained in billets }	AHG
ROUKLOSHILLE	23rd June		Company remained in billets }	

2353 Wt. W2544/1454 700,000 5/15 D. D. & L. A.D.S.S./Forms/C. 2118.

Instructions regarding War Diaries and Intelligence Summaries are contained in F. S. Regs., Part II. and the Staff Manual respectively. Title pages will be prepared in manuscript.

WAR DIARY
or
~~INTELLIGENCE SUMMARY~~.
(Erase heading not required.)

Army Form C. 2118.

Place	Date	Hour	Summary of Events and Information	Remarks and references to Appendices
ROUKLOSHILLE	24th June		Company remained in billets.	AHG
ROUKLOSHILLE	25th June		Company remained in billets. Divisional Horse Show. 1st Prize Single Horse Turnout (Mess Cart) won by Company.	AHG
ROUKLOSHILLE	26th June		Company remained in billets.	JMS
"	27th June		" " " "	JMS
"	28th June		Billeting party to ZEVECOTEN. Billets taken over by 122nd Coy. M.G.C. Capt. M Freeman and all Nos 1 to CANAL - KLEIN ZILLEBEKE Sector to reconnoitre. All Nos 1 remained in the line. Company left billets at 4.10 p.m. Arrived in ZEVECOTEN about 9. p.m.	JMS
ZEVECOTEN IN THE LINE	29th June		Preparations for relief of 72nd Coy. M.G.C. Company left billets to proceed to line at 5.40 p.m. Relief carried out without casualties. Disposition of guns as follows:- (Reference. HILL 60: TRENCH MAP 1/5000.) Left Group:- 2/Lieut. H. WILSON. "A" gun I 36 b 12.15 (KLEIN ZILLEBEKE) "B" gun I 35 a 80.84 } (CATERPILLAR CRATER) "C" " I 35 a 70.80 } "I" " I 36 c 20.14 (RAILWAY).	JMS

Army Form C. 2118.

Instructions regarding War Diaries and Intelligence Summaries are contained in F. S. Regs., Part II. and the Staff Manual respectively. Title pages will be prepared in manuscript.

WAR DIARY
or
~~INTELLIGENCE SUMMARY.~~

(Erase heading not required.)

Place	Date	Hour	Summary of Events and Information	Remarks and references to Appendices
IN THE LINE	June 29th (contd)		Centre Group 2/Lieut. R. Foord Kelcey: 2/Lieut. W. R. Holloway "D" gun I 35 c. 09.90 } (IMPERIAL SWITCH) "E" " I 34 d. 80.85 } "K" " I 35 c. 65.26 } (IMPORTANT TRENCH) "L" " I 35 c 72.40 } Triangular Bluff Group 2/Lieut D. Anderson. "F" gun O. 5 a. 52.32 } (TRIANGULAR BLUFF) "G" " O. 5 a 48.41 } "H" " O. 5 b. 70 64 (BUFF'S BANK) Coy HQ at THE BLUFF 5 guns in reserve (Lieut. C Saxby) Two guns mounted in Anti-Aircraft positions at THE BLUFF	
"	June 30th		Dispositions as for 29th inst. Desultory shelling all day. War diary completed for June 1917.	

[signature] Capt.
Commanding 69th Coy
Machine Gun Corps.

2353 Wt. W2544/1454 700,000 5/15 D. D. & L. A.D.S.S./Forms/C. 2118.

Copy No. 12. APPENDIX "A"

SECRET.

OPERATION ORDER NO. 10 BY CAPTAIN M. FREEMAN
Commanding 69th. Company Machine Gun Corps.

Reference 23rd. Division Operation Map No. 1 Scale 1/5,000 and BELGIUM. Sheet No. 28 N.W. 1/40,000.

1. The 69th. Company Machine Gun Corps will take part in the attack of the 69th. Infantry Brigade on the HILL 60 Subsector.
The Brigade will be supported on the right by the 142nd. Brigade of the 47th. Division and on the left by the 70th. Brigade.

2. The attack will take place at ZERO hour on "Z" day. The dispositions of the Company on "Z" day and the days preceeding it will be as follows:-

"W" Day.	Camp "M". G.17.d.1.6.
"X" Day.	No change.
"X"/"Y" Night.	Move to coppice immediately in rear of MANOR FARM. I.22.c.
"Y" Day.	No change.
"Y"/"Z" Night.	Move to assembly positions as detailed below.

All subsections will be in assembly positions two hours before ZERO.

3. ASSEMBLY POSITIONS:-

(1). Company Headquarters. S.P. 9. I.28.d.40.85.

(2). One subsection No. 1 Section under Lieut. A.H.Graves M.C. in WANGARETTA TRENCH.

(3). One subsection No. 1 Section under 2nd. Lieut. W.R. Holloway in the AUSTRALIAN TUNNELS.

(4). One subsection No. 2 Section under Lieut. H.G.C.Mead in or about GRAND FLEET STREET.

(5). One subsection No. 2 Section under 2nd.Lieut. A. S. Davidson in or about GRAND FLEET STREET.

(6). One subsection No. 3 Section under 2nd.Lieut. D. Anderson in LEEK TRENCH. One gun of this subsection will be mounted in C.6 position. The other gun will be near by in the trench.

(7). One subsection No. 3 Section under Sergt. Mills. in reserve at Company Headquarters.

(8). One subsection No. 4 Section under Lieut. G. W. Symes. M.C. off VERRET RIDE.

(9). One subsection No. 4 Section under 2nd. Lieut. H. Wilson in the AUSTRALIAN TUNNELS.

4. The action of the above guns at ZERO and after will be as follows:-
At ZERO two mines will be fired which will be the signal for the Artillery Barrage to begin:

(1). The subsection under Lieut. A.H.Graves M.C. will fire on the enemy's trenches to the rear of THE SNOUT from ZERO

4. (Contd).

To ZERO plus 2. Fire will only be from one gun, the other gun being kept dismounted in reserve. After the 11th. Batt. West Yorkshire Regiment have left our trenches for the assual Lieut. Graves will report ~~xx~~ at Headquarters 12th. Batt. Durham Light Infantry in ZILLEBEKE SWITCH I.29.d.60.20. This Officer will, with his subsection, move forward with the Headquarters, 12th. Batt. Durham Light Infantry to the forward Command position of that Battalion at I.29.d.60.05. On arrival at this post, if the situation is clear, this Officer will go forward with 4 men carrying Sandbags and shovels and will construct temporary emplacements in the STRONG POINT at I.35.b.90.20 which will be manned by No. 12 Platoon, 12th. Batt. Durham Light ~~xxxxx~~ Infantry. This party will take with them one gun and tripod and two belt boxes.
When these positions are constructed Lieut. Graves will send back his party to the forward Command Post of ~~te~~ 12th. Batt. Durham Light Infantry. This party will then bring forward the remaining gun and all gun stores which will be mounted in the emplacements referred to above. The duty of these two guns will be to assist in the consolidation of this STRONG POINT and in the repelling of any counter attacks which may take place.

(2). The subsection under 2nd. Lieut. W.R. Holloway will move at ZERO minus 20 out of the Tunnel in to BENSHAM AVENUE. Immediately after the explosion of the mines the two guns of this Subsection will take up the normal defensive positions in LARCH WOOD L.11., and INFANTRY TUNNELS L.1. These guns will be purely defensive and will be held in reserve. This subsection will probably be ordered to move forward to assist in consolidation of STRONG POINTS in rear of the final objective east of the CUTTING.

(3). The subsection under Lieut. H.G.C.Mead will move forward to assist in the consolidation of the front lip of the new CATERPILLAR CRATER about I.35.a.90.60.
Lieut. H.G.C.Mead with 3 Orderlies will move forward with the two Platoons of "C" Company, 8th. Batt. Yorkshire Regiment which will occupy the CATERPILLAR CRATER. As soon as Lieut. Mead considers it practicable for his two guns to move forward he will send back two orderlies to guide the guns in to their positions.
As soon as the last wave of the Infantry have left our front line these two guns will move in to the front line where they will wait for the Orderlies who will guide them to their positions.
The orderlies must know the exact point in the trench where the teams will be waiting, and the N.C.O. in charge of the teams will keep a vigilant look out for these orderlies. These guns will assist in the consolidation of the CRATER and will remain there until orders to move are received from Company Headquarters.

(4). The subsection under 2nd. Lieut. A.S. Davidson will move forward to the junction of IMPACT SUPPORT and IMPACT AVENUE, I.35.a.40.10, and will assist in the consolidation of a STRONG POINT to be made there.
2nd.Lieut. Davidson with 3 orderlies will move forward in rear of "A" Company, 10th. Batt. Duke of Wellingtons Regt., and will select positions for his two guns. As soon as this Officer considers it practicable for his guns to move forward he will send two orderlies to guide the Guns. As soon as the last of the Infantry have left our front line these guns will move up in to the front line where they will await the arrival of the orderlies. The orderlies must know the exact position in the front line which the guns will take up and the N.C.O. in charge of teams must keep a vigilant look out for the Orderlies.

(5). The subsection under 2nd. Lieut. D. Anderson will remain in their defensive positions until orders are received from Company Headquarters.
In all probability this subsection will be ordered to move forward to assist in the consolidation of a STRONG POINT to be made by the 9th. Batt. Yorkshire Regiment about I.35.d.15.30.

(6). The subsection under Sgt Mills will remain in Company Reserve, and will probably be ordered to move forward to assist in consolidation of STRONG POINTS immediately in rear of the final objective on the front of the 9th. Batt. Yorkshire Regiment, probably at JUNCTION of IMPACT CRESCENT and IMPACT TERRACE. I.35.d.60.75.

(7). The subsection under Lieut. G.W. Symes will move forward to assist in the consolidation of STRONF POINTS to be formed by 11th. Batt. West Yorkshire Regiment at the junction of IMP AVENUE and IMP SUPPORT (I.29.d.50.40)
Lieut. Symes will move forward with 3 orderlies with "D" Company, 11th. Batt. West Yorkshire Regiment and will select positions for his two guns. As soon as this Officer considers it practicable for his guns to move forward he will send two orderlies to guide the teams.
As soon as the last of the Infantry have left our front line these guns will move forward to the front line where they will await arrival of the Orderlies. The Orderlies must know the exact positions in the front line which the teams will take up and the N.C.O. in charge of teams must keep a vigilant look out for the orderlies.

(8). The subsection under 2nd. Lieut. H. Wilson will move forward to assist in the consolidation of the CRATER to be formed on HILL 60. 2nd. Lieut. H. Wilson will move forward with 3 orderlies with the 2 platoons of "C" Company 8th. Yorkshire Regiment which will occupy this Crater.
At ZERO minus 20, these teams will move to BENSHAM AVENUE where they will remain till the mines have exploded.
Immediately after the explosion of the mines the teams will move forward up SWIFT STREET to the Front Line where they will await the arrival of the orderlies from 2nd. Lieut. Wilson.
As soon as this Officer considers it practicable for his guns to move forward he will send two orderlies to guide the teams.
The orderlies must know the exact position in front line to be occupied by these guns and the N.C.O. in charge of guns will keep a vigilant look out for the orderlies.

(9). Officers commanding subsections will be informed by their Orderlies whenever Company Headquarters moves, and the position to which it has moved.

(5). REPORTS
Subsection Officers will report immediately to Company Headquarters by their H.Q. Orderly when their guns are in position after any move. The headquarter orderly will remain at Headquarters and another orderly will be sent with him who will return to his subsection Officer.
All messages will be sent in duplicate.
The Headquarter Orderly of each subsection will always be sent to his subsection Officer with any orders to move.
This orderly will move with the subsection to its new position and will be sent back to Headquarters with the message reporting completion of move.

(6). INTER-COMMUNICATION.
Immediately on arrival at a new position subsection Officers

will get into communication with the Headquarters of the Battalion with whom they are operating and with the subsections on their right and left. The forward Command positions of Battalions are as under:-

10th. West Riding Regiment.	I.35.a.50.40.
8th. Yorkshire Regiment.	I.35.b.10.90.
11th. West Yorkshire Regiment	I.29.d.55.45.
9th. Yorkshire Regiment.	I.35.b.00.20.
12th. Durham Light Infantry.	I.29.b.60.95.

Runner relay posts will be established at the following points:-

X relay post.	I.35.a.00.70.	
Y relay post.	I.29.c.65.45	(SWIFT STREET)
Z relay post.	I.29.d.25.55.	

6. FIGHTING KIT.

The fighting kit to be carried will be as follows:-

On the man Steel Helmet, haversack on back, waterbottle filled, entrenching tool, waterproof sheet, tube helmet, box respirator, field dressing, 2 Sandbags, 2 Mills grenades (one in each bottom pocket of S.D. jacket), 12 rounds revolver ammunition. Each rifleman will carry 50 rounds rifle ammunition. 48 hours rations.

Each Gun Team will carry the following equipment, Gun, Tripod, 12 Belt boxes, spare parts, first aid case, supply of 4 x 2., condenser bag and tube, spare barrel, cleaning rod, two shovels, 2 petrol cans of drinking water, 2 petrol cans of water for gun.

7. All ranks must co-operate in every way with the Infantry with whom they are working, and will always take greatest care to ensure thatbthey do not impede the movements of the Infantry.

8. Administrative Orders regarding supply of water, rations, S.A.A. etc. will be issued separately.

32/12

[signature]
Lieut & Adjutant.
69th. Company Machine Gun Corps.

No. 69
MACHINE GUN
COMPANY.
No.
Date 3-6-17

SECRET

AMENDMENT NO. 1 TO OPERATION ORDER No. 10 BY
CAPTAIN M. FREEMAN, COMMANDING 69th. Coy. M.G.Corps.

Sub para 2 od para 3 ASSEMBLY POSITIONS, should now read

1 Subsection No. 1 Section under Lieut. A.H.Graves. M.C. will remain in COPPICE immediately in rear of MANOR FARM, I.22.c until ZERO plus 2 hours, when it will move forward to Headquarters pf 12th. Batt. Durham Light Infantry as detailed in para 4., sub para 1.

Lieut. & Adjutant.
69th. Company Machine Gun Corps.

APPENDIX "B"

SECRET.

69th. COMPANY MACHINE GUN CORPS.

REPORT ON ATTACK OF HILL 60 COVERING PERIOD FROM 7th.June 1917 to 13th.June 1917.

The dispositions of the Company in the assembly positions were complete by 1-0a.m. 7th. June 1917.
These dispositions were as follows:-
Company Headquarters. S.P. 9.

(a). GUNS DETAILED FOR FIRST OBJECTIVE.
1 Subsection of No. 2 Section under 2nd.Lieut. A.S.Davidson off GRAND FLEET STREET.
1 Subsection of No. 2 Section under Lieut. H.G.C.Mead off GRAND FLEET STREET.
1 Subsection No. 4 Section under 2nd.Lieut. H. Wilson in the AUSTRALIAN TUNNEL.
1 Subsection No. 4 Section under Lieut. G.W.Symes M.C. off VERRET RIDE.

(b). GUNS DETAILED FOR BLUE AND BLACK LINES.
1 Subsection No. 3 Section under 2nd.Lieut. D.Anderson in M.G. positions C.6 and L.10.
1 Subsection No. 1 Section under Lieut. A.H.Graves M.C. in the COPSE by the south side of ZILLEBEKE LAKE.

(c). RESERVE GUNS.
1 Subsection ~~xxxxx~~ No.3 Section under Sergt. H. Mills in reserve at Company Headquarters S.P. 9.
1 Subsection of No. 1 Section under 2nd.Lieut. W.R.Holloway in the AUSTRALIAN TUNNEL (M.G. positions L.1 and L.11).

THE ATTACK.
The Officers Commanding the subsections detailed in "A" above moved forward to the attack immediately in rear of the first wave of the attacking Infantry and on reaching the positions, for the garrisoning of which they had been detailed, sent back runners to bring up their guns.

2nd. Lieut. A.S. Davidson moved forward with "A" Company, 10th. Batt. Duke of Wellington's Regiment under Lieut. Perks D.S.O. This Officer reached the Strong Point at I.35.a.40.10 without casualties and sent back for his guns which also arrived without casualties, and were mounted in position by 4-20a.m. Under orders of O.C., 10th. Batt. Duke of Wellington's Regiment these guns were moved to positions from which they could protect the right flank of this Battalion. These guns did not fire as the situation did not demand it.

Lieut. H.G.C.Mead moved forward from the diagonal in rear of the first wave of the Company of the 8th. Batt.Yorkshire Regiment commanded by Captain Pearson M.C. This Officer and 1 orderly reached the CATERPILLAR CRATER from which position the orderly was sent to bring up the guns, which were reported in position by 4-20a.m.
One of this Officers orderlies was not seen after leaving our front line and is believed to have been killed.
One of the orderlies sent back by this Officer to report that his guns were in position was wounded on the way to Company Headquarters.
No. 10017, Pte. Robert Davies of this subsection was wounded in the wrist while carrying his load of ammunition to the objective. This soldier carried his load right up to the position and attempted to assist in digging the emplacement until ordered to the Dressing Station.

2nd. Lieut. H. Wilson moved forward in rear of the first wave of "C" Company, 8th. Batt. Yorkshire Regiment under Capt. Atkinson, and reached the HILL 60 CRATER without casualty. From this position he sent orderlies to bring up his guns from SWIFT STREET. One gun reached the CRATER at ZERO plus 23 minutes, the other gun proceeded too far, eventually reaching the CRATER about an hour later. No. 9477 Pte. TATE M. was wounded in the right hand while carrying his gun up to the position. He carried his gun right forward however, and took part in constructing the emplacement until ordered to go to the Dressing Station.

Lieut. G.W.Symes M.C., went forward with the first wave of "D" Company, 11th. Batt. West Yorkshire Regiment under Capt. C.L.Armstrong M.C., and reached the German support line at I.29.d.50.35.
Before reaching this position this Officer encountered a small party of the enemy who were obstinately resisting, and with the help of No. 43743 Pte. Sugden A. dispersed them, killing four. This Officer than sent back for his guns which were reported in positions near I.29.d.43.30 and I.29.d.48.36 by 4-15a.m.
Owing to both Lieut. Symes' orderlies becoming casualties no message was sent back to fetch the guns for about three-quarters of an hour.
No. 8899 Pte. Chase T. volunteered to go out during the barrage in search of this Officer and eventually found him, and again returned through the barrage to bring forward the guns.

All the above guns, which were the guns detailed for the first objective, reached the positions to which they had been detailed and were in action in improvised emplacements before ZERO plus one hour and a quarter.

2nd. Lieut. D. Anderson with his subsection went forward, as arranged, with Headquarters of the 9th. Batt. Yorkshire Regiment and remained with them until the situation was clear when he moved forward to a position just forward of the blue line at I.35.central. These guns had been originally intended to occupy the Strong Point at I.35.d. 15.20., but as the situation was not clear and under instructions from O.C., 9th. Yorkshire Regiment, 2nd.Lieut. D. Anderson took up position at I.35. central.
This subsection suffered no casualties.

Lieut. A.H.Graves M.C. and his subsection moved from the COPSE near ZILLEBEKE LAKE at ZERO and proceeded to Headquarters, 12th. Batt Durham Light Infantry in ZILLEBEKE SWITCH.
This subsection suffered 3 casualties when passing through the enemy barrage near STREAM CORNER. On arrival at Battalion Headquarters this subsection moved forward with the Headquarter party of the Battalion to advanced Battalion Headquarters where Lieut. Graves M.C. left his teams and guns, going forward himself with orderlies to select and construct a position. Finding the strong point at I.35.b.90.20. untenable this Officer placed one of his guns in the front line at about I.36.c.2.9. and one about 150 yards in rear of the front line at about I.36.c.10.95 firing across the railway in to BATTLE WOOD.
At about 9p.m. this Officer moved his guns back to the Strong Point at I.35.b.90.20.
This subsection lost 3 men killed in addition to those wounded already mentioned.

The reserve subsection under Sergt. Mills moved forward sooner than was intended, owing to an Orderly misunderstanding a message which had been given to him, to Headquarters 9th. Batt. Yorkshire Regiment from which place it moved to a position at about I.35.d.30.40.

No firing took place by any Guns of this Company with the exception of No. 3 Section, each subsection of which fired 500 rounds to the south west of KLEIN ZILLEBEKE at about Square I.36.d. on S.O.S. on Z/A night.

All the above guns remained in their positions until the 9th inst. On the morning of this day the subsection under Lieut. Graves M.C. was relieved by the subsection under 2nd. Lieut. W.R.Holloway from the TUNNEL. The reason for this relief was that Lieut. Graves' subsection had been subjected to heavy shelling at intervals throughout the period and had worked very hard with weakened teams under very trying conditions.
During the evening of this day under instructions from Brigade Headquarters the following reliefs and withdrawals took place:-
Company Headquarters were moved to GRAND FLEET STREET and LEEK TRENCH.
2 Subsectionsof 68th. Company Machine Gun Corps relieved the twonsubsections in the CRATERS, which subsections were withdrawn to reserve at LEEK TRENCH. This relief was complete at 11p.m. Belt boxes and tripods were handed over in each case.

During the period 9th. to 12th., the enemy shelling increased especially from the direction of HOOGE, both CRATERS and the SNOUT receiving special attention from this quarter.
LEEK TRENCH and GRAND FLEET STREET also received attention, shells landing at regular intervals throughout the day and night.

On the 11th inst., Company Headquarters and reserve teams moved to S.P. 9.
The same evening the subsection under 2nd.Lieut. A.S. Davidson relieved the subsection under 2nd.Lieut. W.R.Holloway, which subsection in turn relieved the subsection under Lieut. G.W.Symes M.C. who withdraw with his subsection to reserve in INFANTRY TUNNELS.
On the same evening the subsection under Lieut. A.H. Graves M.C. moved at 9-30p.m. from INFANTRY TUNNEL to relieve one subsection of 68th. M.G.Coy. in the HILL 60 CRATER. Owing to very heavy shelling on the way the relief was not complete until 2a.m.
On the same evening the subsection under Lieut. H.G.C. Mead moved from S.P. 9 at 9-20p.m. to relieve one subsection 68th. Coy M.G.Corps in the CATERPILLAR CRATER. Relief was complete about 12 midnight.

The Company was relieved on the night 12th/13th. by the 17th.Coy. M.G.Corps. The Commanding Officer of this Company visited me at my Headquarters at 12 noon and arranged all details of relief. Owing to casualties it was not found possible to take Belt boxes out with the Company. These were accordingly handed over and an equivalent number drawn from Transport Lines of 17th. Company.
Owing to heavy shelling the relief was delayed and was not complete until 4-30a.m.
At about 4-0a.m. 5566 C.S.M.Woolmer R. was wounded by a premature burst from one of our 18pdrs.
I wish to put on record the excellent work done by this Warrant Officer throughout the operations. He displayed untiring energy and devotion to duty in carrying out his duties, and on many occasions performed acts of gallantry which were not necessarily included in his duties.

I desire to draw attention to the excellent work of all ranks of the Machine Gun Corps. All ranks performed their duties conscientiously and cheerfully throughout the whole tour under trying circumstances; teams had

been greatly depleted through casualties throwing increased work on all; in spite of the fact that the men were very tired all ranks carried out any deed which was assigned to them xxxxxx thoroughly and cheerfully.
Special mention is made of the excellent work done by men employed as runners. These men often worked throughout the day carrying messages through heavy shell fire and in no case did any man who was unwounded fail to deliver a message.

The total casualties suffered by the Company including attached men were 36 O.R's.

NOTES AND SUGGESTIONS.

The method employed of co-operation with the Infantry of sending forward the subsection Officer and orderlies in advance with the first wave proved highly successful in every case.

The method of carrying ammunition and gun stores, though each man had a heavy load, was found to work satisfactorily. Sufficient material was carried to ensure that even though 2 or 3 men of the team became casualties sufficient stores would be left with the gun to enable fire to be opened and maintained until the stores could be completed from the reserve of 32 belt boxes which were maintained at Company Headquarters. No attempt was made to form small dumps of S.A.A. as it was thought that these would be difficult to find and liable to be destroyed. Subsections in every case drew from the Headquarters of the Battalions with which they were working. 2,000 rounds S.A.A. in boxes were collected for each gun and handed over on relief.

The desirability of increase in the establishment of a Machine Gun Company was emphasized during the operations. It was found that the men attached from the Infantry, with the exception of a few, took very little interest in the work of the Company. These men had not had time to become thoroughly acquainted with their Officers and comrades and it is thought that considerably better results would be obtained were it possible for a Machine Gun Company to go into action without any men specially attached.

No Yukon packs were issued to this Company for the operations, and it is thought that these would prove of great value.

The utility of packsaddlery was again brought out. The whole of the gun equipment in addition to rations and water was carried up on pack transport without a single casualty to animals and without difficulty. On several occasions the pack column passed through Gas Shells., horse respirators proving effective.

Captain.
Commanding 69th. Company Machine Gun Corps.

Copies to:-
69th. Infantry Brigade.
Xth. Corps Machine Gun Officer.
Divisional Machine Gun Officer.
2 for War Diary.
2 for File.

APPENDIX. C

69th Company Machine Gun Corps

Regtl No	Rank & Name			Unit	Nature of Casualty	Remarks
12515	Pte	Bruce	W	8th Yorks	Killed in Action	
22819		Fullbrook	J	M G C	-do-	
12477		Grant	R W	-do-	-do-	
12113		Kirkpson	E	11th West Yorks	-do-	
72687		Newton	J	M G C	-do-	
35888		Penn	M	M G C	-do-	
72699		Stewart	D	M G C	-do-	
27625		Ashworth	C	8th Yorks	Wounded in Action	
16090		Bradley	H	9th Yorks	Wounded in Action	
34988		Burns	G	8th Yorks	-do-	
5586		Bird	S	M G C	-do-	
28022		Bromby	W	M G C	-do-	
41124		Cartwright	G	11th West Yorks	-do-	
35733		Kirkshaw	J	M G C	-do-	
28177		Campbell	F	M G C	-do-	
10017		Dawes	R W	M G C	-do-	
40192		Fose	H	10th West Riding	-do-	
23130	L/Cpl	Farquharson	J	M G C	-do-	
51096	Pte	Partridge	J	M G C	-do-	
23316		Hall	C	M G C	-do-	
10155		Kendall		2nd West Riding	-do-	
11657		O'Grady	J	-do-	-do-	
36069		Oram	G	M G C	-do-	
142874		Owens	G	8th Yorks	-do-	
92676		Pamment	F	M G C	-do-	
38027		Parsons		8th Yorks	-do-	
72702		Stocks	J	M G C	-do-	
43703		Sugden	A	11th West Yorks	-do-	
23120		Stockdale	J	M G C	-do-	
12791		Walker	A	10th West Riding	-do-	
11597		Wankless	E	9th Yorks	-do-	
[illegible]	C.S.M.	Wallner	R	M G C	-do-	
	Lieut.	AHGraves MC		MGC	do at Duty.	

[illegible] Capt.
Comdg 69th Coy MGC

Army Form C. 2118.

WAR DIARY
or
~~INTELLIGENCE SUMMARY.~~
(*Erase heading not required.*)

Instructions regarding War Diaries and Intelligence Summaries are contained in F. S. Regs., Part II. and the Staff Manual respectively. Title pages will be prepared in manuscript.

69 M G Coy
Vol 18

Place	Date	Hour	Summary of Events and Information	Remarks and references to Appendices
BLUFF	July 1st		Company remained in trenches } During this period hostile artillery was	A.H.G.
BLUFF	July 2nd		Company remained in trenches } fairly active especially during the early	A.H.G.
BLUFF	July 3rd		Company remained in trenches } morning. Hostile aeroplanes displayed	A.H.G.
BLUFF	July 4th		Company remained in trenches } great boldness frequently flying over our trenches	A.H.G.
~~[illegible]~~			at a very low altitude & firing machine guns at working parties etc	A.H.G.
~~STEENVOORDE~~			These aeroplanes were frequently engaged by machine gun fire but without effect.	
			Company relieved by 141st Coy M. G. C. Owing to hostile shelling	
STEENVOORDE	July 5th		the relief was not complete till about 5.0 a.m. on 5/7/17. On relief	
			company proceeded by lorries to billets in the STEENVOORDE area,	
			arriving about 7.30 am.	A.H.G.
STEENVOORDE	July 6th		Company remained in billets at near STEENVOORDE. MILITARY MEDALS AWARDED by CORPS COMMANDER to the undermentioned men,	
			85107 Pte HARDEN, J 10017 Pte DAVIS R.W.	
			9477 Pte TATE H 14827 Pte GUY	
			8906 Pte RUSSELL C.H, 43743, Pte SUGDEN	
			BAR to MILITARY MEDAL awarded to No 23127 Sgt COWLING W.	

2353 Wt. W2544/1454 700,000 5/15 D. D. & L. A.D.S.S./Forms/C. 2118.

Army Form C. 2118.

Instructions regarding War Diaries and Intelligence Summaries are contained in F. S. Regs., Part II. and the Staff Manual respectively. Title pages will be prepared in manuscript.

WAR DIARY
or
INTELLIGENCE SUMMARY.

(Erase heading not required.)

Place	Date	Hour	Summary of Events and Information	Remarks and references to Appendices
STEENVOORDE	July 7th		Company remained in billets near STEENVOORDE	
STEENVOORDE	July 8th		Company remained in billets near STEENVOORDE BAR TO MILITARY CROSS awarded to Lt A.H. GRAVES M.C MILITARY CROSS awarded to Capt. M. FREEMAN DISTINGUISHED CONDUCT MEDAL awarded No 5566 CSM. R. WOOLLER Authority X Corps 4R.23 dated 6/7/17.	A.H.G.
STEENVOORDE	July 9th		Company remained in billets near STEENVOORDE.	A.H.G.
STEENVOORDE	July 10th		Company remained in billets near STEENVOORDE	A.H.G.
STEENVOORDE	July 11th		Company remained in billets near STEENVOORDE	A.H.G.
STEENVOORDE } MICMAC CAMP }	July 12th		Company marched from STEENVOORDE area to tents near MICMAC CAMP arriving about 6 p.m.	
MICMAC CAMP ~~STEENVOORDE~~ H31 central (Sheet 28)	July 13th		Company remained in tents near MICMAC CAMP. Six gun teams under Lt A.H. GRAVES M.C., 2/Lt A. BISHOP and 2/Lt R. FOORD KELCEY and Nos 1 & 2 of all gun teams proceeded to the trenches. Relief of teams of 68th M.G.C. carried out as follows. Four gun teams: One team I 30 d. 6.30. one team at	

Army Form C. 2118.

Instructions regarding War Diaries and Intelligence Summaries are contained in F. S. Regs., Part II. and the Staff Manual respectively. Title pages will be prepared in manuscript.

WAR DIARY
or
~~INTELLIGENCE~~ SUMMARY.
(Erase heading not required.)

Place	Date	Hour	Summary of Events and Information	Remarks and references to Appendices
MICMAC CAMP	July 13th		I 30 d 20 00 two gun teams at KLEIN ZILLEBEKE I 36 b 30.60 under Lt A.H. GRAVES M.C at I 30 d 60 30. Two guns at ~~I~~ I 30 c 95.80 under 2/Lt R. FOORD KELCEY at I 30 d. 00.90. In addition to officers Nos 1 & 2 proceeded to their positions with guns and tripods. The remainder under 2/Lt A. BISHOP remained at S.P. 9 I 28 d 30 95. (Reference Map Sheet ZILLEBEKE 1/10,000)	AHG
MICMAC CAMP HILL 60	July 14th		Company Headquarters and remainder of Company relieved 68th M.G.C. in the HILL 60 Subsector. Relief was not complete till about 4.20 am owing to congestion of traffic on roads, hostile shelling & the difficulty of reaching positions. On Completion of relief dispositions in addition to those described above was as follows. Company Headquarters at LARCH WOOD. 3 Gun teams in reserve at SP 9 (reserve & barrage positions) under 2/Lt W.R. HOLLOWAY at S.P. 9	

2353 Wt. W2544/1454 700,000 5/15 D. D. & L. A.D.S.S./Forms/C. 2118.

Instructions regarding War Diaries and Intelligence Summaries are contained in F. S. Regs., Part II. and the Staff Manual respectively. Title pages will be prepared in manuscript.

WAR DIARY
or
INTELLIGENCE SUMMARY.
(Erase heading not required.)

Army Form C. 2118.

Place	Date	Hour	Summary of Events and Information	Remarks and references to Appendices
HILL 60.	July 15th		Four gun teams in the SNOUT at I29d 40.30, I29d 60.30, I29d 80.60, I29d 65.60 under 2/Lt D. ANDERSON at I29d 35.30: 3 gun teams in ~~[illegible]~~ HEDGE STREET TUNNELS at I30d 45.85, I30d 80.20, I30d 30.60, under Lt C. SAXBY. In addition to the above 10 guns 70th M.G.C. were attached to the Company for barrage purposes, — as follows: 4 gun teams at CORNER HOUSE, 4 gun teams on VERBRANDENMOLEN ROAD, 2 gun teams at S.P. 9.	AHS
HILL 60	July 16th		Company remained in trenches in the HILL 60 SUBSECTOR / During this	
HILL 60	" 17th		Company remained in trenches in HILL 60 SUBSECTOR / period hostile artillery was	
HILL 60	" 18th		Company remained in trenches in HILL 60 SUBSECTOR / exceedingly active on our	
HILL 60	" 19th		Company remained in trenches in HILL 60 SUBSECTOR / trenches & in back areas, both	
HILL 60	" 20th		Company remained in trenches in HILL 60 SUBSECTOR / day and night mainly from	
HILL 60	" 21st		Company remained in trenches in HILL 60 SUBSECTOR / guns of heavy calibre. Firing	
HILL 60	" 22nd		Company remained in trenches in HILL 60 SUBSECTOR. / was mainly from the S. & S.E. & at times reached great intensity, especially between 10 a.m. & 5 p.m.	

2353 Wt. W2544/1454 700,000 5/15 D. D. & L. A.D.S.S./Forms/C. 2118.

Instructions regarding War Diaries and Intelligence Summaries are contained in F. S. Regs., Part II. and the Staff Manual respectively. Title pages will be prepared in manuscript.

WAR DIARY
or
INTELLIGENCE SUMMARY.
(Erase heading not required.)

Army Form C. 2118.

Place	Date	Hour	Summary of Events and Information	Remarks and references to Appendices
HILL 60	July	22nd	Our own artillery bombarded enemy trenches with guns of all calibre. Harassing fire was carried out nightly by machine guns of the company, as many as 14,000 rounds being fired a night. SAA was also carried up to Barrage positions of the 24th DIVISION by carrying parties from Transport lines at MICMAC CAMP. There was great aerial activity on both sides & many air fights took place. The enemy made great use of gas shells especially on our back areas. Areas on the Brigade front which were most heavily shelled were MOUNT SORREL, TOR TOP, Squares I 30 d & I 36 b, THE SNOUT, LARCH WOOD and S.P. 9. Direct hits were frequently obtained on British and German Ammunition dumps & had it not been for the concrete dugouts the Company would have suffered very heavy casualties from the accuracy of the German fire. Total casualties were 2 men killed, 3 wounded and 3 gassed.	
			Four guns under Lt A.H. GRAVES M.C. were relieved on the night	

Army Form C. 2118.

Instructions regarding War Diaries and Intelligence Summaries are contained in F. S. Regs., Part II. and the Staff Manual respectively. Title pages will be prepared in manuscript.

WAR DIARY
or
~~INTELLIGENCE SUMMARY.~~
(Erase heading not required.)

Place	Date	Hour	Summary of Events and Information	Remarks and references to Appendices
HILL 60	July 22nd		of July 21/22 ~~the relief was carried~~ by 4 guns ~~73~~ 72nd B.M.G.C. Relief was complete by 4.0 am ~~morning~~ 22nd. Remainder of Coy & Coy H.Q. were relieved on the night 22/23. by guns of 17th, 72nd 73rd and 191st M.G. Coys.	A.H.G.
MICMAC CAMP (H.31 central Sheet 28)	July	23rd	Relief was complete by 6 am 23rd. On relief all teams & Coy H.Q. proceeded to MICMAC CAMP. Company paraded at 3.30 pm & marched to billets in the METEREN AREA at R32 d. 80.20. (Reference Map Sheet 27)	A.H.G.
METEREN	July 24th		Company remained in billets.	A.H.G.
METEREN	July 25th		Company remained in billets. Inspection by G.O.C. 23rd Division at 11 am at H.Q. 11th Bn West Yorkshire Regt. (R 32 c. 80.00)	A.H.G.
METEREN PETIT DIFQUES	July 26th		Company entrained at CAESTRE at 11 am & proceeded by train to St OMER arriving about 1.30 pm. Company then marched to billets at PETIT DIFQUES arriving 4.40 pm.	A.H.G.
PETIT DIFQUES	July 27th		Company remained in billets at PETIT DIFQUES } During this period training	
PETIT DIFQUES	July 28th		Company remained in billets at PETIT DIFQUES } was carried out by Sections	
PETIT DIFQUES	July 29th		Company remained in billets at PETIT DIFQUES } in GUN DRILL MECHANISM	

2353 Wt. W2544/1454 700,000 5/15 D. D. & L. A.D.S.S./Forms/C. 2118.

Instructions regarding War Diaries and Intelligence Summaries are contained in F. S. Regs., Part II. and the Staff Manual respectively. Title pages will be prepared in manuscript.

WAR DIARY
or
INTELLIGENCE SUMMARY.
(Erase heading not required.)

Army Form C. 2118.

Place	Date	Hour	Summary of Events and Information	Remarks and references to Appendices
PETIT DIFQUES.	July 25th		Company remained in billets at PETIT DIFQUES } FIRING (30 yds range).	
PETIT DIFQUES	July 2[illegible]th		Company remained in billets at PETIT DIFQUES. } Specialists also trained in	
PETIT DIFQUES	August 1st		Company remained in billets at PETIT DIFQUES. SCOUTING, RANGEFINDING. YUKON PACK, SIGNALLING	
			War diary Completed for July 1917.	A.H.S.

[signature]
Captain
Commanding 69' Company M. G. Corps

2353 Wt. W2544/1454 700,000 5/15 D. D. & L. A.D.S.S./Forms/C. 2118.

Instructions regarding War Diaries and Intelligence Summaries are contained in F. S. Regs., Part II. and the Staff Manual respectively. Title pages will be prepared in manuscript.

WAR DIARY
or
INTELLIGENCE SUMMARY.
(Erase heading not required)

Army Form C. 2118.

69 M G Coy

Vol 19

Place	Date	Hour	Summary of Events and Information	Remarks and references to Appendices
PETIT DIFQUES	Aug 1st + 2nd		Coy remained in billets.	J.A.S.
PETIT DIFQUES	Aug 3rd		do. Coy baths at HOULLE 2/Lt A BISHOP to METEREN to DIVISIONAL GAS SCHOOL for gas course (Aug. 2nd)	J.A.S.
do.	Aug. 4th.		Coy remained in billets. Billet work carried out owing to heavy rains.	J.A.S.
do	Aug 5th		do. Divine service parades.	J.A.S.
do	Aug 6th.		do. Specialist training in Yukon Pack team work, Range finding + signalling. Remainder: - indirect fire by map + use of dials, map reading + compass work, and attached men training in packsaddlery drill, belt filling + musketry	J.A.S.
do	Aug. 7th		do. Intersection competition:- (a) Inspection in Fighting Order, (b) Firing on range (c) Section Yukon Pack teams (d) Belt filling for attached men. Transport:- (a) Inspection (b) Driving drill (c) Driving through pegs (d) Alarm.	J.A.S.

2353 Wt. W2544/1454 700,000 5/15 D. D. & L. A.D.S.S./Forms/C. 2118.

Instructions regarding War Diaries and Intelligence Summaries are contained in F. S. Regs., Part II. and the Staff Manual respectively. Title pages will be prepared in manuscript.

WAR DIARY
or
INTELLIGENCE SUMMARY.
(Erase heading not required.)

Army Form C. 2118.

Place	Date	Hour	Summary of Events and Information	Remarks and references to Appendices
PETIT DIFQUES.	Aug.	8th	Coy. remained in billets. Range work for Nos 1 + 2. Specialist instruction as before. Remainder:- Packsaddlery drill, gas drill, gun drill + section drill	[initials]
PETIT DIFQUES to LE BAS de MOULLE	Aug.	9th	Morning. Coy. parades as usual Afternoon. Coy. moved from PETIT DIFQUES to LE BAS de MOULLE. arrived in new billets about 4.30 p.m.	[initials]
LE BAS DE MOULLE	Aug.	10th	Coy. remained in billets. 15. O.R transferred to 194th Coy M.G. Corps (Authority 23rd DIV. No A/2839/72 of 4 8 17.) 2/Lt A BISHOP rejoined from DIV. Gas School + qualified as a Gas Officer	[initials]
do	Aug.	11th.	Coy. remained in billets. Parades:- Coy drill, gun drill + practising men in map reading + compass work Lt. A. H. GRAVES. M.C to Divisional M G School as Instructor (Aug 10th)	[initials]
do	Aug.	12th	Brigade Church Parade at 10 a.m at HOULLE. Captain Mr Freeman MC preached the sermon 2/Lt. R TAYLOR reported from Base Depot (11th August)	[initials]
do	Aug.	13th	Coy. remained in billets. Tactical scheme on Training Area for officers and Sergeants during morning. No 2 Section on range	

2353 Wt. W2544/1454 700,000 5/15 D. D. & L. A.D.S.S./Forms/C. 2118.

Instructions regarding War Diaries and Intelligence Summaries are contained in F. S. Regs., Part II. and the Staff Manual respectively. Title pages will be prepared in manuscript.

WAR DIARY
or
INTELLIGENCE SUMMARY.
(*Erase heading not required.*)

Army Form C. 2118.

Place	Date	Hour	Summary of Events and Information	Remarks and references to Appendices
LE BAS DE MOULLE	Aug 13th		during afternoon, firing classification practices	[initials]
do	Aug 14th		No 4 Section on range at PETIT DIFQUES all day, for firing classification practices. Attached men's class under 2/Lt HOLLOWAY. Remainder of Company on Training area	[initials]
do	Aug 15th		No 3 Section on range all day, firing classification practices. Remainder of Company on Training area practising deployment from line of march, & advancing in attack formation on a given line. 2/Lt. D ANDERSON to 18th Corps Infantry School VOLKERINCHOVE.	[initials]
do	Aug 16th		No 1 Section on range all day, firing classification practices. Remainder of Coy parade at Transport lines for intensive digging by sections, gun drill ceremonial drill, etc. Specialist training for signallers & range finders. Lieut A.H Graves MC proceeded to join M.G.T.C. Struck off strength accordingly.	[initials]
do	Aug 17th		No 2 Section on range all day firing classification practices. Remainder of Coy. revolver practice on range, gun drill from limbered wagons, action from pack animals, etc. 9.30 p.m. Whole company paraded for night marching.	[initials]

2353 Wt. W2544/1454 700,000 5/15 D. D. & L., A.D.S.S./Forms/C. 2118.

Army Form C. 2118.

Instructions regarding War Diaries and Intelligence Summaries are contained in F. S. Regs., Part II. and the Staff Manual respectively. Title pages will be prepared in manuscript.

WAR DIARY
or
INTELLIGENCE SUMMARY.
(Erase heading not required.)

Place	Date	Hour	Summary of Events and Information	Remarks and references to Appendices
LE BAS DE MOULLE	Aug 18th		Coy. remained in billets. 2/Lt D ANDERSON rejoined from 15th Corps School	[signature]
do	Aug 19th		Whole coy. paraded 7.0 a.m for Brigade Field Firing at GUEMY. Covering fire from flanks, during an attack, practised. Returned to billets about 8 p.m	
do	Aug 20th.		Coy. remained in billets. Belt. filling during morning. Baths at HOULLE during afternoon. 8 p.m. Brigade night exercise, forming up on tapes	[signature]
do	Aug. 21st.		Coy. paraded 8.0 a.m for Brigade exercise on training area. Returned to billets 4 p.m. 5 p.m. Brigade Aquatic Sports at HOULLE	[signature]
do	Aug. 22nd.		Coy. remained in billets.	[signature]
do.	Aug. 23rd.		do. All Transport left at 3 p.m to proceed to WIPPENHOEK area.	[signature]
do & near ABEELE	Aug. 24th		9.0 a.m. Coy. left billets - marched to WATTEN STATION and entrained at 1 p.m for ABEELE. Detrained at 5 p.m and reached new billets at K 35 a 9.9 (Sheet 27) near ABEELE at 6 p.m	[signature]
do	Aug. 25th.		Company moved to DICKEBUSCH area. Company without transport embussed near ABEELE at 4.30 p.m. Transport moved later by	

2353 Wt. W2544/1454 700,000 5/15 D. D. & L. A.D.S.S./Forms/C. 2118.

Army Form C. 2118.

Instructions regarding War Diaries and Intelligence Summaries are contained in F. S. Regs., Part II. and the Staff Manual respectively. Title pages will be prepared in manuscript.

WAR DIARY

~~or~~

~~INTELLIGENCE SUMMARY.~~

(Erase heading not required.)

Place	Date	Hour	Summary of Events and Information	Remarks and references to Appendices
			ward. Company arrived in Camp near CAFE BELGE (Sheet 28 N.W. H29a) about 8 pm.	MF
DICKEBUSCH.	26.8.17		Company remained in Camp. Lieut Toynbee and 2/Lt Holloway reconnoitred front to be taken over. Captain M. Freeman M.C. rejoined from leave.	MF.
DICKEBUSCH	27.8.17.		Company remained in Camp. Captain M. Freeman M.C. and Lieut G. W. Symes M.C. reconnoitred front to be taken over.	MF.
DICKEBUSCH	28.8.17.		Company remained in Camp. 2/Lt H. Wilson reconnoitred front.	MF
DICKEBUSCH	29.8.17.		Company remained in Camp. 2/Lt A. Bishop reconnoitred front.	MF.
DICKEBUSCH	30.8.17.		Company remained in Camp. 2/Lt R. F. Kelley and 2/Lt R. T. Taylor reconnoitred front.	MF.
DICKEBUSCH.	31.8.17.		Company remained in Camp. Sergt Mills and Sergt Leach reconnoitred front. G.O.C. 69 Infantry Brigade inspected the camp.	MF.
DICKEBUSCH.	1.9.17		War Diary for August 1917 completed.	MF.

M. Freeman, Captain
Commanding 69 Company M. G. Corps.

2353 Wt. W2544/1454 700,000 5/15 D. D. & L. A.D.S.S./Forms/C. 2118.

No. 69
MACHINE GUN
COMPANY.
No. ✓
Date 4.10.17.

To
Staff Captain
69. Inf Brigade

Attached please find War Diary duly completed for the month of September 1917.

[signature]
Captain
COMDG. No. 69 M. G. COY.

69/23

Army Form C. 2118.

Instructions regarding War Diaries and Intelligence Summaries are contained in F. S. Regs., Part II. and the Staff Manual respectively. Title pages will be prepared in manuscript.

WAR DIARY
or
~~INTELLIGENCE SUMMARY~~.
(Erase heading not required.)

69 M G Coy
Vol 20

Place	Date	Hour	Summary of Events and Information	Remarks and references to Appendices
DICKEBUSCH	1-9-17		Company remained in Camp near DICKEBUSCH.	[illegible]
STEENVOORDE	2-9-17		Company marched from DICKEBUSCH to STEENVOORDE	[illegible]
LEDERZEELE	3-9-17		Company marched from STEENVOORDE to LEDERZEELE.	[illegible]
LEDERZEELE	4-9-17		Company remained in Billets.	[illegible]
-do-	5-9-17		Company remained in Billets.	[illegible]
-do-	6-9-17		Company remained in Billets.	[illegible]
-do-	7-9-17		Company remained in Billets	[illegible]
-do-	8-9-17		Company remained in Billets.	[illegible]
-do-	9-9-17		Company remained in Billets. 2/Lt D. ANDERSON reconnoitred front.	[illegible]
	10-9-17		Company remained in Billets Lieut C. [illegible] reconnoitred front. [illegible]	
-do-	11-9-17		Company remained in Billets. Two N.C.O's reconnoitred front	
-do-			Sgt Kennedy W. L/Cpl Ross T.B	[illegible]
-do-	12-9-17		Whole company paraded 8-30 am for Brigade exercise, returned to	
-do-			billets about 3-30 pm. Two N.C.O's reconnoitred front. Sgt Lewis L/Cpl Kernent	[illegible]
-do-	13-9-17		Company marched from LEDERZEELE to STEENVOORDE area.	[illegible]
STEENVOORDE	14-9-17		Company marched from STEENVOORDE to ONTARIO Camp.	[illegible]
ONTARIO CAMP RENINGHELST.	15-9-17		Company remained in Camp.	[illegible]

Army Form C. 2118.

WAR DIARY
or
~~INTELLIGENCE SUMMARY~~.
(Erase heading not required.)

Instructions regarding War Diaries and Intelligence Summaries are contained in F. S. Regs., Part II. and the Staff Manual respectively. Title pages will be prepared in manuscript.

Place	Date	Hour	Summary of Events and Information	Remarks and references to Appendices
MICMAC CAMP	16-9-17		Company marched to MICMAC Camp.	[illegible]
-do-	17-9-17		Company remained in Camp. Four Anti-Air Craft gun positions made & manned.	[illegible]
-do-	18-9-17		Lt. C. Sassly + 7 OR's proceeded to Reinforcement Camp at MICMAC Camp. Lieut G. W. Symes M.C + 2/Lieut. R. Foord-Kelcey with No IV section proceeded to the line.	[illegible]
-do-	19-9-17		Remainder of Company & H.Q proceeded to the line.	[illegible]
STIRLING CASTLE.	20-9-17		Company in the trenches. Operation orders attached.	[illegible]
	21-9-17		Company remained in trenches.	[illegible]
	22-9-17		Company remained in trenches.	[illegible]
	23-9-17		Company remained in trenches	[illegible]
	24-9-17		Company relieved in the line by the 98th & 100 Coy. M.G.C. relief orders attached.	[illegible]
ONTARIO CAMP.	25-9-17		Detailed list of Casualties from the 19-9-17 to 25-9-17 attached. Company proceeded to ONTARIO CAMP.	[illegible]
	26-9-17		Company remained in Camp. 8 O. Ranks joined for duty from base Depot.	[illegible]

2353 Wt. W2544/1454 700,000 5/15 D. D. & L. A.D.S.S./Forms/C. 2118.

Instructions regarding War Diaries and Intelligence Summaries are contained in F. S. Regs., Part II. and the Staff Manual respectively. Title pages will be prepared in manuscript.

Army Form C. 2118.

WAR DIARY
or
~~INTELLIGENCE SUMMARY~~.
(Erase heading not required.)

Place	Date	Hour	Summary of Events and Information	Remarks and references to Appendices
ONTARIO CAMP	27-9-17		Company proceeded to the line. Casualties Sgt. Cowling W.23137 killed in action. 23124 Cpl G. Carr wounded in action.	[illegible]
	28-9-17		Company remained in trenches. 2/Lieut A.C. Higgins + 20 O. Ranks reported for duty from base depot.	[illegible]
	29-9-17		Company remained in trenches.	
	30-9-17		No change in situation. Company occupying same positions till evening when 2 guns at BLACK WATCH CORNER were withdrawn owing to very heavy casualties among 1 team 2/Lt Bishop and Pte Hinchcliffe being wounded and 4 men killed.	[illegible]
	1-10-17		Company remained in line. War Diary for September completed.	[illegible]
			Appendices. (a) Operation Order No 26	
			(b.) Administrative Arrangements in connection with O.O. 26.	
			(c.) Detailed list of Casualties from 19.9.17 to 25.9.17	
			(d.) Operation Order No 27.	
			(e.) Detailed list of casualties from 27.9.17 – 2.10.17	
			(f) Report on action of Company from 19.9.17 – 23.9.17.	

[illegible signature]

[illegible] 9 . 15

Appendix A

[illegible]

Commanding [illegible] Machine Gun [illegible]

[illegible] 23rd Division [illegible] Operation Map [illegible]

[illegible]

[illegible]

1. The [illegible] Company Machine Gun Corps will [illegible] part in the attack [illegible] Infantry Brigade on the left of the 2nd [illegible] Brigade will be supported on the right by [illegible] Infantry Brigade, on the left by the [illegible] Australian Brigade 1st Australian Division.

2. The attack will take place at Zero hour on "ATTACK DAY" [illegible] "E" Day.

3. The disposition of the Company [illegible] ZERO hour will be as follows:–

(a) Company Headquarters in dugout [illegible]

(b) [illegible] sub-section of No. I Section under 2nd Lieut. H Bishop in Assembly trenches of right half of "D" Coy. [illegible] West Yorkshire Regt. [illegible] [illegible] ER AVENUE.

(c) A subsection of No. IV Section under Lieut. G.W. Sykes M.C. in Assembly trenches [illegible] "D" Coy. 11th Battn. [illegible] Yorkshire Regt. north of JASPER AVENUE.

(d) [illegible] section of No. II Section under 2nd Lieut. W.R. Holloway in assembly trenches of "[illegible]" Coy. [illegible] West Yorkshire Regt. [illegible] [illegible] R LANE.

(e) [illegible] section of No. III Section under 2nd Lieut. R.T. Taylor in assembly trenches of No. 13 Platoon, "D" Coy. [illegible] Yorkshire Regt. situated south of JASPER LANE. [illegible] attached [illegible] to the above platoon [illegible] [illegible] RAILWAY DUGOUTS.

(f) A subsection of No. III Section under 2nd. Lt. D. Anderson in dugouts near Company Headquarters.

(g) A subsection of No. I Section under Sgt. J. Keach in dugout near Company Headquarters.

(h) A subsection of No. IV Section under 2nd. Lieut. R. Ward-Kelsey in normal defensive position in JASPER AVENUE

(i) A subsection of No. I Section under 2nd. Lieut. W. Wilson in normal defensive position in Strong Point to the south of JASPER LANE at J.13.d.90.55 (approx)

The action of the above subsections at and after ZERO hour will be as follows:-

(a) Company Headquarters will remain at STIRLING CASTLE unless otherwise notified.

(b) The subsection under 2nd. Lieut. A. Bishop will move forward in rear of the right half of "D" Coy., 11th. West Yorkshire Regt. and will assist in the consolidation and garrisoning of Strong Point B at HEREMTHAGE CHATEAU, J.20.b.20.80.

(c) The subsection under Lieut. G.W. Symes M.C. will move forward in rear of the left half of "D" Coy, 11th. West Yorkshire Regt. and will assist in the consolidation and garrisoning of Strong Point C. at AID POST, J.20.b.60.90.

(d) The subsection under 2nd. Lieut. W. R. Holloway will move forward in rear of "A" Coy., 11th West. Yorkshire Regt. and will assist in the consolidation and garrisoning of Strong Point "E" the CHATEAU at J.14.d (central)

(e) The subsection under 2nd Lieut. R.T. Taylor will move forward with No. 13 platoon, "D" Coy of 9th Yorkshire Regt. and will assist in the consolidation and garrisoning of Strong Point I at the TOWER J.14.d.95.40

(f) The subsection of No. III Section under 2nd. Lieut D. Anderson will move forward from Company Headquarters to the Headquarters of 10th. Duke of Wellingtons at entrance to JASPER AVENUE at [illegible] in time to advance with the H.Q. party of his Battalion at Zero plus 3 hours to the Strong Point I at J.[illegible].

The subsection of No. 1 Section under Sgt. Leach will move forward with 2nd. Lieut. D. Anderson and will be under the command of this Officer until the Strong Point I is reached. On arrival at Strong Point I. 2nd. Lieut. D. Anderson will obtain a guide from the 10th Duke of Wellington's to guide him to Strong Point "P" at NORTHAMPTON FARM. J.[illegible].90. where he will make a reconnaissance of the ground and select positions for the four guns which he will move forward as soon as he considers it practicable.

2nd. Lieut. D. Anderson will arrange for Sgt. Leach to be similarly guided to Strong Point "H" at J.21.b.10.90 which he will eventually garrison. This N.C.O will act throughout as detailed above for 2nd. Lt. D. Anderson.

6. REPORTS

Subsection Officers will report immediately to Company Hdqrs. by their H.Q. orderly when his guns are in position after any move. After his arrival with the first report the H.Q. orderly will remain at Headquarters. The man sent with him will return to his Subsection Officer. The H.Q. orderly of each subsection will always be sent to his subsection Officer with any orders to move. This orderly will move with the subsection to its new position, and will be sent back to Headquarters with the message reporting completion of move.

All messages will be sent in duplicate. It is most important that the time and place should always be included on the message. Message forms on back of operation map should be used when available, and position of guns and any other useful information marked on the map.

6. INTERCOMMUNICATION.

Immediately on arrival at a new position Subsection Officers will get into communication with the Headquarters of the Company and Battalion with whom they are operating and with the subsections on their right and left. The forward Command positions of Battalions are as under:-

11th. Batt. West Yorkshire Regt: J.13.b.70.70.
9th " Yorkshire Regt: J.20.b.80.90.
10th " Duke of Wellington's: J.14.d.90.40
8th " Yorkshire Regt: J.13.d.40.10.
Advanced report centre, 11th West Yorks: J.14.a.45.45

2nd Lieut. W.R. Holloway will arrange to get into touch with the M.G. of the 2nd Australian M.G. Coy. at FITZCLARENCE FARM.

2nd. Lieut D. And-son will arrange to get into touch with M.G. of same Company [illegible] about J.15.a.55.10.

2nd Lieut A. Bishop will arrange to get into touch with Subsection of 68th Company under Sgt. Cole at Strong Point at J.20.b.50.40.

Lieut G.W. Symes M.C. will arrange to get into touch with the subsection of 68th Company above and also subsection of same Company under Lieut Smith at KANTINTJE CABARET - J.21.a.60.40.

Sgt Leach will arrange to get into touch with the subsection of 68th M.G. Coy under 2/Lieut R.F. Smith at J.21.b.40.50.

7. FIGHTING KIT

The fighting Kit to be carried will be as follows:-

On the man:- Steel helmet, haversack on back, waterbottle filled, entrenching tool, waterproof sheet, tube helmet, box respirator, field dressing: 2 Sandbags, 2 Mills Grenades (one in each bottom pocket of S.D. Jacket) 18 rounds Revolver ammunition. Each rifleman will carry 50 rounds

The ammunition – 48 hours rations.
Each gun team will carry the following
[illegible] box [illegible] first aid case, [illegible] spare [illegible] condenser bag & tube, spare barrel, cleaning rods, [illegible] shovels, 2 petrol cans [illegible] water, 1 petrol can [illegible] water for gun.

6. Co-operation. All ranks must co-operate in every way with the Infantry with whom they are working and must always bear [illegible] in mind to ensure [illegible] to complete the movements of the Infantry.

7. Administrative orders regarding supply of ammunition, rations, S.A.A. etc. will be issued separately.
Orders for concentration march and dispositions prior to ZERO DAY will be issued separately.

J. W. H. [illegible] Capt. & Adjutant
[illegible] Coy. Machine Gun Company.

17-9-17.

Copy No 1 2nd Lieut A. Bishop — 9 [illegible] Corps.
2 Lieut C. W. Symes M.C. — 10 [illegible] Coy. M.G. Corps.
3 2nd Lt W. R. Holloway — 11 Brigade Major [illegible] Infantry Brigade
4 2nd Lt R. T. Taylor — 12 D.M.G.O. [illegible] Division
5 2nd Lt D. Anderson — 13 Corps M.G.O. [illegible] Corps
6 Sgt. Leach — 14 War Diary.
7 2nd Lt R. [illegible] — 15 War Diary.
8 2nd Lt H. Wilson — 16 File.

(10–13) For information

Copy No. 4. SECRET.

Appendix B

Administrative Arrangements in connection with Operation Order No 26 by Capt. M. Freeman M.C., Commanding 69th Company Machine Gun Corps.

1. Rations Each man will proceed to the line with 48 hours rations in addition to his Iron Rations. These rations are for consumption on the 20th. and 21st inst. Rations for consumption on the 22nd. inst will be issued from Company Headquarters. No. 4 Section in addition to the above have been issued with rations for the 19th. in bulk.

2. WATER. Each gun team will carry into the line two petrol cans of drinking water and one petrol can for guns, in addition to each man's filled water bottle. Greatest care is to be taken to prevent the waste of water.
All orderlies coming to Hdqrs. will always bring any empty water bottles or tins for refilling. These will be returned filled, with tea if possible.
No receptacle for water is on any account to be dumped. It must be preserved until it can be filled at the nearest water point.

3. S.A.A. A dump of S.A.A. is established at STIRLING CASTLE. Arrangements are being made for half boxes of S.A.A. to be sent up as soon as possible.

4. MEDICAL: Aid Posts and Advanced Dressing Stations are established as follows:-

(a) Regimental Aid Posts

CLAPHAM JUNCTION.	J.13.d.90.80.
STIRLING CASTLE	J.13.d.40.00.
JACKDAW AVENUE.	J.13.c.55.15

(b) Advanced Dressing Stations:-

MENIN ROAD.	I.29.b.90.60
WOODCOTE HOUSE	I 20.c.40.28.

5. RETURNS. The following returns are required daily:
1 p.m. Casualties from 12 noon previous day: exact numbers to be reported if possible: otherwise numbers estimated.
If any casualties are received during the night they must be reported to Company Headquarters by 5 a.m. next morning.
Demands for ammunition may be sent at any time.
Recommendations for Immediate Awards to be sent as soon as possible after the action for which commended, care being taken to give full christian names.
Times at which situation reports are required will be notified later. A short statement of the situation should be sent with every man going to H.Q.

6. Transport Officer will collect as much salvage as possible and return to Salvage Dumps. All ranks will return salvage when possible.

7. Transport Officer will keep a list of any men who may be sent to him from Straggler's Post. These men will be sent at once to Brigade Reinforcement Camp with orders to report as Stragglers to the Commandant. A duplicate list will be forwarded to Brigade Headquarters.

J. W.H. Toynbee Lieut & Adjutant
69th Coy. Machine Gun Corps

13-9-17.

Copy No. 1. 2/Lieut. A. Bishop.
2. Lieut G.W. Symes M.C.
3. 2/Lieut W.R. Holloway
4. 2/Lieut R.T. Taylor
5. 2/Lieut. D. Anderson
6. Sgt. G. Leach
7. 2nd Lt. H. Wilson
8. 2nd Lt. R. Foord-Kelsey
9. Transport Officer
10. War Diary
11. War Diary
12. File

No. 69 Coy. M. Gun Corps Appendix "C"

Detailed List of Casualty's from 19.9.17 to 25.9.17

Reg. No	Rank & Name		Unit	Nature of Casualty	Date of Casualty	Remarks
	2/Lieut	W. R. Holloway	M. G. C.	Killed in Action	20.9.17.	
3640	Pte	Bidgood S. W.	— —	— —	19.9.17.	
90779	"	Atkinson W.	— —	— —	20.9.17	
85168	"	Jenkins G.	— —	— —	20.9.17	
8901	"	Moore J.	— —	— —	21.9.17	
235359	"	Garrett A.	9/Batt Yorkshire Regt	— —	19.9.17	
15618	"	Taylor J.	M. G. C.	— —	24.9.17.	
23133	C/pl	Hoggard H.	— —	Wounded in Action	20.9.17.	
89820	Pte	Allison W. C	— —	— —	20.9.17	
72675	"	Williamson J.	— —	— —	20.9.17	
72699	"	Mitchell J. A	— —	— —	20.9.17.	
15617	"	Tasker W. J	— —	— —	20.9.17	
28233	"	McLean H	9/Batt Yorkshire Regt	— —	20.9.17	
266316	"	Nicol J.	10/Batt Duke of Wellington	— —	20.9.17.	
5612	"	Standill W.	M. G. C.	Missing	20.9.17.	
87837	"	Brown F	— —	Wounded at Duty	21.9.17.	
72692	"	Wise C.	— —	— —	21.9.17.	
	2/Lieut	H. Wilson	— —	— —	22.9.17.	
72691	Pte	Hinchcliffe A	— —	— —	22.9.17.	
97703	"	Green F. C.	— —	— —	22.9.17.	
8396	L/C/pl	Donnelly F	— —	Wounded in Action	22.9.17.	

Appendix "D"

[illegible]

Reference ZILLEBEKE [illegible] 1/10,000

I [illegible] relieve [illegible]
[illegible]
[illegible] Coy [illegible] attached [illegible]
[illegible]

II [illegible]
and [illegible] transport [illegible]
Section [illegible] transport [illegible]
[illegible] Coy H.Q. [illegible]

III [illegible] will
be brought [illegible]
unit orders will be handed over
[illegible]
[illegible]
possible information [illegible]
over to relieving officers and
teams.

IV Transport officers will detail
[illegible]
[illegible] the junction of [illegible] Rd
and ZILLEBEKE [illegible]
at the times stated — Row

Operation Order No 27 (continued)

Sheet II.

IV (contd.)

(a) One limber containing [illegible] gun carts for eight guns and ten tripods of [illegible] sections 4-0 pm

(b) One half limber containing four gun carts for guns, and tripods of [illegible] sections under [illegible] and [illegible] leaving at 6-0 pm

(c) One half limber containing four gun carts for guns and tripods of [illegible] sections under [illegible] and [illegible] leaving at 10-0 pm

All limbers will proceed via DERBY Rd SHRAPNEL CORNER and WARRINGTON RD.

V The Transport Officer will arrange to draw belt boxes from Companies as under:—

(a) 40 Belt Boxes from 10[illegible] M.G. Coy at Transport lines [illegible] to-night

(b) 120 Belt Boxes from Transport lines of 9[illegible] M.G. Coy, [illegible] by [illegible]

Operation Order No 27 (continued)

Sheet III

VI The following will be relieved [illegible]
[illegible]

(a) [illegible]
H.Q. (A) [illegible]
(b) [illegible]
(c) Sub section [illegible]
(d) [illegible]
[illegible]
[illegible]
over
[illegible]
[illegible]

Relief for (c) will [illegible] from
H.Q. [illegible] will arrive at your position
about 3.30 pm

Relief for (d) will leave H.Q at 6.30 pm

VII The following will be relieved
by [illegible]

(a) Sub section under [illegible]
Relief will leave H.Q about
6.30 pm

Operation Order No 27 (continued)

Sheet II

VII (continued)

(b) Sub section under Sgt G Manning will leave H.Q. about 2.0 pm.

The C.S.M. will detail two men to be at Transport Farm at 12.0 Noon to guide relieving sections of 100 M.G. Coy to H.Q.

VIII No guides will be required from sections.

IX The Q.M. will arrange for hot meal to be ready for all sections on arrival at MIC MAC Camp.

[illegible] Lt & Adjt
[illegible] Coy M.G. Corps

Copies to:—

1 Lt G.W. Seymour M.C.
2 2/Lt A Bishop
3 " I Anderson
4 " H Wilson
5 " R Ford-Kelsey
6 Sgt G Manning
7 O.C. [illegible] M.G. Coy
8 Transport Officer
9 War Diary
10 File

Appendix 'E'

No. 69 Coy M. Gun Corps

Detailed list of Casualties from 27.9.17 to 2.10.17.

Reg No.	Rank & Name		Unit	Nature of Casualty	Date of Casualty
	2/Lieut	A. Bishop	M. G. C.	Wounded in action	29. 9. 17
23127	Sgt.	Cowling W.	— " —	Killed in action	27. 9. 17.
23124	Cpl.	Carr J.	— " —	Wounded in action	27. 9. 17.
5626	Pte	Collins G.	— " —	Killed in action	29. 9. 17
34064	"	Millward R.	— " —	— " —	29. 9. 17.
88036	"	Swindells H.	— " —	— " —	29. 9. 17
39262	"	McCarthy J.	8/Batt Yorkshire Regiment	— " —	29. 9. 17.
72691	"	Hinchcliffe A.	M. G. C.	Wounded in action	29. 9. 17.
35006	"	Nicholls W.	— " —	Wounded at Duty	1. 10. 17

Appendix "F"

Action of 69th Company Machine Gun Corps from the night 19th/20th to 23rd September 1917.

The Company arrived in its Assembly positions at 9-30p.m. on the 19th September. The subsections were distributed as under:

(a) 2nd. Lieut A. Bishop with one subsection with right half of "D" Coy. 11th West Yorks Regt. in the right of New Cut Trench.

(b). Lieut G.W. Symes M.C. with one subsection with the left half of "D" Coy, 11th West Yorks in New Cut Trench.

(c) 2nd Lieut W. R. Holloway with one subsection with "A" Coy, 11th West Yorks. in JASPER LANE.

(d) 2nd Lieut. R. T. Taylor with one subsection with "D" Coy 9th. Yorks in the GRID TRENCH.

(e) 2 Lieut D. Anderson with one subsection at Company Hdqrs. STIRLING CASTLE

(f) Sgt. Leach with one subsection at Company Hdqrs.

(g). 2nd. Lieut R, Toord-Kelcey with one subsection in normal defensive position in JAM RESERVE and JASPER AVE.

(h) 2 Lieut H. Wilson with one subsection at J.13.d.90.65. in defensive positions

Coy. Headquarters with the 10th Duke of Wellington's at STIRLING CASTLE.

At Zero hour the subsections mentioned in paras (a), (b), (c), (d) and (e) moved forward with the platoons they were working with to the following Strong Points:–

2nd. Lieut Bishop to HERENTHAGE CHATEAU. This Officer met with no difficulties, the teams followed in rear of the platoon detailed for the consolidation of the Strong Point and were only checked for a very short period by enemy M.G. fire from the Copse. Two men lost touch with the teams whilst going through the Copse, one of whom rejoined the following day. The other man is still missing, believed to be slightly wounded and evacuated.

The guns were mounted and positions dug quickly and without

difficulty, no more casualties being suffered until the evening of the 31st when a very heavy barrage was opened along the red line one being Killed.

Lieut. Symes M.C. lost two men of his subsection just b one leaving the assembly trench, both being Killed instantaneously. He found no difficulty in reaching his strong point at the AID POST where he mounted one gun at each side of the MENIN ROAD. The gun north of the MENIN ROAD was moved later in the afternoon to a position just south of the other gun.

Though these positions were heavily shelled no further casu ties occurred in the subsection.

2nd. Lieut. W. R. Holloway's subsection was not so successful in reaching its objective, the strong point at the CHATEAU, J. 14. d. 55. 60. as the two subsections above mentic ed, owing to 2/Lt. Holloway being Killed whilst preparing to leave the assembly trench. The teams went too far forward and had to return being eventually placed in position by Lieut Symes. This subsection also had a trying time from shell fire, having 4 men wounded.

2nd. Lieut R. T. Taylor's subsection encountered no difficulties in getting to its objective, the strong point at the TOWER J. 14. d. 95. 15. Whilst at this point the subsection were very heavily shelled and was ordered to move further forward inti the Blue line but owing to a misunderstanding the teams were given a guide for the right of the Green line. They never reached this point as their guide lost them.

At this period 2nd. Lieut. Taylor put his teams into a dugout near by (which in the morning proved to be in VELDHOEK) and returned to the Duke of Wellington's Hdqrs. for another guide.

No guide was available and this Officer started back to return to his teams. He did not reach them and was found the following morning lying in a shell-hole in a semi-conscious state near the above Headquarters. The subsection was found the next morning and one team was placed in the Blue Line and the other sent forward to replace a gun in the Green Line which had been destroyed.

The part taken in the action by the subsection under 2nd. Lieut. D. Anderson is described in the attached report by this Officer.

The subsection under Sgt. Leach followed the H.Q. party of the 10th. Duke of Wellington's Regt. from STIRLING CASTLE to Strong Point I., the TOWER. This subsection was detailed to proceed to the right flank of the Brigade in the Green Line.

This subsection by a misunderstanding occupied a position in STRONG POINT "N" at J.21.b.15.90., which was the original point for which this subsection had been detailed. The N.C.O. reported himself in position in the Green Line and it was only discovered on the following morning that the subsection was in the Strong Point "N". Accordingly I ordered 2nd. Lt. Bishop to report to O.C., 10th Duke of Wellington's. I instructed this Officer to obtain a guide to "A" Coy, 10th. D. of W's. and to make a thorough reconnaissance of the ground with a view to moving this subsection forward into the Green Line at dusk. This was carried out with the exception that only one gun was moved forward, the other gun having been destroyed by shell fire at S.P. "N" on the afternoon of the 21st. Sept.

This gun was replaced on the morning of the 22nd. by a gun belonging to 2nd. Lieut. Taylor's subsection as recorded above.

On the 22nd. Sept. the Brigade front was altered and the following moves and reliefs

Report of Action of No. 5 Subsection, 69th M.G. Company from Sept 20th to Sept 24th 1917.

This subsection came into the line with the remainder of the Company in the afternoon of Sept 19th and was accommodated in dugouts near STIRLING CASTLE at J.19.b.60.80.

A subsection from No. 6 Section under Sgt. Leach shared the same dugouts as it was intended that these two subsections should operate together in the initial stages of the days operations. Batt H.Q. of the 10th D. of W's. West Riding Regt. were in the same area and from the outset close touch was kept with this Battalion.

At 5 a.m. on the morning of the 20th, 4 runners, two from each subsection, were attached to the Signalling Officer of the West Ridings who intended to move forward behind the 9th Yorkshire Regiment to the Blue Line. This Officer moved into position in NEW CUT shortly before Zero so as to be in front of the enemy's barrage. The runners started off from this trench shortly after Zero, saw the Blue Line captured, noted the exact location of STRONG POINT I. and returned without casualties about ½ hour after Zero to the teams at STIRLING CASTLE.

At Zero+3 hours I moved forward with the C.O., West Riding Regiment to his new H.Q. at Strong Point I. At the same time, the teams started off from their dugouts in charge of the runners and reached STRONG POINT I without casualties and complete with all stores about twenty minutes after I arrived at this point.

From now onwards Sgt. Leach's subsection ceased to be under my Command.

From Strong Point I, it was possible to observe the capture and consolidation of the Green Line. When the work of consolidating commenced I at once moved forward with Sgt. Kennedy. We found that NORTHAMPTON FARM to which place operation orders detailed the subsection to go was useless as a vantage points for machine guns. Positions were therefore selected along a line of dugouts - J.15.d.50.75 about 100 yds behind the line being consolidated by the Infantry. An excellent command of the valley of the REUTELBEEK as well as a reasonable clearance over the heads of the infantry was got by selecting positions on the top of the dugouts. Sgt Kennedy at once returned to STRONG POINT I to bring up the teams.

While the work of consolidation was proceeding and pending the arrival o the teams, I reported to Capt. Lilley, 8th Yorkshire Regt. I also got into touch with the Machine Gun Company of the Brigade on our left and it was arranged that one of their guns should protect the right bank of the REUTELBEEK and that one of mine should shoot across their front on the left bank of the stream. Throughout the operations a most cordial understanding existed between the Infantry and Machine gunners on both banks of the river.

At Zero + 1½ hours my teams reached their positions without casualties and complete with ammunition and all stores. Guns were at once got into position and shortly afterwards the enemy were observed massing in the Cemetery in ZWAANHOEK. They were out of range to our guns but were promptly dealt with by artillery. Parties of about 20 then began to deploy on both banks of the REUTELBEEK at about J.16.c.60.85. Our guns at once opened fire effectively dispersing these parties and inflicting many casualties. Two men on the right gun team were wounded by snipers from their right rear. I at once ordered the position to be changed to a more protected one in front of the dugouts.

took place:-

The subsection at the AID POST was withdrawn to reserve at CLAPHAM JUNCTION.

The subsections at HERENTHAGE CHATEAU, BLUE LINE and right of the GREEN LINE were relieved by six guns of the 194th Coy. M.G. Corps. and were drawn into reserve at CLAPHAM JUNCTION and JAM RESERVE trench.

The subsection under 2nd Lieut. R. Foord-Kelcey moved from JAM RESERVE to FITZCLARENCE FARM in relief of 2 guns of [illegible] Australian M.G. Coy.

Subsection under 2nd Lieut. H. Wilson moved from JASPER LANE near CLAPHAM JUNCTION to a position about J.q. 60.10. near BLACK WATCH CORNER in relief of 2 guns of 2nd Australian M.G. Coy.

The subsections under 2nd Lt. [illegible] Anderson and Sgt. Manning remained in position making 8 guns in the line and 8 in reserve.

These were the positions occupied by this Company on the 23rd Sept.

[illegible signature] Captain
Commanding 69th Coy. M.G. Corps.

30-9-17.

This movement in the valley continued for some hours, the enemy attempting to deploy in smaller parties, all these were dispersed. Many casualties were inflicted on the enemy, the number being estimated at between 250 and 300. Many dead were seen lying about. From 4 pm. 20th September onwards enemy movement in this area was reduced to a minimum. Strict orders were given that all parties were to be fired on. What was probably an F.O.O's party about J.16.a.60.10 was dispersed: a party of about 20 men near J.17.c.80.85 was fired on and several casualties inflicted. A ration party of about 10 near J.16.d.50.90 was fired on on the morning of Sept. 21st. and nearly all Killed. From thence onward all movement ceased except in the case of a party of eight bearing a Red Cross Flag. This was dispersed by fire from the machine gun company on our left.

From Sept. 20 till the teams were relieved on the afternoon of Sept. 24 no further counter attack was made but artillery fire was at times very heavy. L/Cpl. Melvin's gun being once buried and finally on Sept. 24 completely Knocked out.

No difficulty was experienced in getting up rations and water a party of 3 being dispatched each morning to Coy. Hdqrs. immediately after the artillery fire which developed each morning as dawn had died away.

The teams were relieved on the afternoon Sept 24 by a subsection of the 100th. M.G. Coy. The relief was conducted amid considerable hostile artillery fire and Pte. Taylor was unfortunately Killed.

It should be put on record that throughout these operations the spirit and enthusiasm of the men were splendid and that their unceasing vigilance in the front line was characterised by an extraordinary cheerfulness.

D Anderson 74
69th. M. Gun Coy.

30-9-17.

23rd Div.S.G.181/1/2.

68th Infantry Brigade.
69th Infantry Brigade.
70th Infantry Brigade.
194th Machine Gun Coy.

Would you please have the attached form filled in by your Machine Gun Company and returned to this office when completed.

Two copies of statements made by prisoners relating to effect of Machine Gun Barrage are enclosed.

23rd Division.
26th Sept.1917.

for Lieutenant-Colonel,
General Staff.

BM 615/22

"A" Form.
Army Form C.2121
(In pads of 100).

MESSAGES AND SIGNALS.

No. of Message

Prefix .... Code MS ....m. | Words 22 | Charge

Office of Origin and Service Instructions.

fd

Sent
At 2.34 p.m.
To [illegible]
By

This message is on a/c of: .... Service.

(Signature of "Franking Officer.")

Recd. at ....m.
Date
From
By

TO 69th Bde

Sender's Number.	Day of Month.	In reply to Number.	AAA
* GB176	4		

My	SG181/1/2	of	26th	Sept
aaa	Please	hasten	reply	re
MG	action	on	Sept	20th

From
Place 23rd Div.
Time

The above may be forwarded as now corrected. (Z)

Censor. Signature of Addressor or person authorised to telegraph in his name.

* This line should be erased if not required.

750,000. W 2186—M509. H. W. & V., Ld. 5/16.

Copy.

O.C. 69th Machine Gun Company.

Will you please fill up the attached form and return to this Office by 12 noon on the 28th inst.

One copy of statements made by prisoners relating to effect of machine gun barrage is enclosed.

E.R. Appleyard
Capt.,
for Brigade Major.
69th Infantry Brigade.

H.Q. 69th Inf.Bde.
September 26th,1917.
B.M.615/22.

6th/577 expedite

The following Statements were made by Prisoners as to the effect of our M.G. Barrage on September 20th :-

1. A Corporal in the German support line said that he was in a dugout with 12 or 15 men. At first they were not under M.G. fire, but after the attack had started, very heavy M. G. fire came down upon the trench, killed the sentry, and played direct upon the dugout, preventing him and his men coming out.

2. A similar statement as to the effect of M. G. fire was made by a man on the right of the MENIN Road, and by a man in a dugout East of TOWER HAMLETS.

3. A platoon with a light machine gun in a sunken road on the front of the 39th Division was prevented from coming into action by M.G. fire.

4. A prisoner stated that he was in a dugout in the second line. The cry was raised " The English are coming ", and he ran about a hundred yards & found himself under M. G. fire. He lay in a shell hole till he was captured.

Copy to 69th Bde GC

Xth Corps Machine Gun Officer,
25/9/1917.

(1)

O.C. 69th Machine Gun Company.

Will you please fill up the attached form and return to this Office by 12 noon on the 28th inst.

One copy of statements made by prisoners relating to effect of machine gun barrage is enclosed.

[signature] Appleyard
for Capt.,
Brigade Major.
69th Infantry Brigade.

H.Q. 69th Inf.Bde.
September 26th,1917.
B.M.615/22.

(2) Brigade Major
69th Infantry Brigade

Attached form is returned duly completed as requested. Delay in forwarding same is regretted, please.

[signature] Captain
Commanding 69th Company M.G. Corps.

3.10.17.

? Correspondence

O.C. 69 M.G. Coy

X CORPS
MACHINE GUN
OFFICER.
No. ....
Date 25-9-17

Please give **short** account of your action on ~~June~~ Sept 20 etc.

~~7th - 8th~~, and answer the following questions :-

Method employed.	Lesson learnt.
1. Composition and equipment of team.	Teams consisted of 7 men and carried: Gun, Tripod, First Aid case, 10 Belt boxes (each man carrying three) 2 shovels and 2 tins of water. Each man carried on the average 4 sandbags and 2 Mills bombs. [as extra supply] 4 x 2 and kit was carried with each team.
2. Ammunition supply (forward dumps, carrying parties, amount required, method of carrying.)	Forward dumps were not established. From a reserve of 80 belt boxes at Company HQ the runners returning from teams in the line took forward belt boxes to replace any which did not arrive at the objective. No carrying parties were required in addition to the 32 infantry attached for instruction. Three boxes per man were carried.
3. Water supply	Each team carried 2 petrol tins of water; empty tins were sent by runner to Company H.Q. and replaced by full tins obtained from Brigade Dump in exchange for empty tins.
4. Replacement of casualties and repair of guns.	Each team sent back 2 men on arrival at objective (after consolidation) being teams of 5 per gun. These and men from teams in reserve were used to replace casualties. 2 new guns and tripods were drawn from D.A.D.O.S before going into action. All damaged guns were repaired by artificer, where possible; if he could not repair them they were repaired by

Divisional Armourer

5. Method of advance. (by bounds: on whose order: etc.)	Teams advanced immediately in rear of the platoons detailed to consolidate the strong point to which guns had been allotted. Teams conformed throughout to movements of these platoons.
6. Selection of objective and siting of gun. any direct targets?	Objectives were all detailed in Brigade Operation Orders. Guns were sited so as to obtain cross fire to cover the front in case of counter attack. Direct targets were engaged. (See report from 2/Lt Anderson, attached)
7. Liaison with Infantry.	Subsection Commanders worked throughout with the commanders of the infantry companies with whom they advanced
8. Communication with Coy. H.Q.	Each subsection had two runners who advanced with it. One afterwards returned to Company H.Q. and took all messages from there to his own subsection. The orderly with the subsection was responsible for communication back to Company. H.Q.
9. Barrage Companies - Any improvements in methods to suggest ?.	Report on action is attached

[signature] Captain

Commanding 69th Company M G Corps

3.10.17.

Method employed.	Lesson learnt.
1. Composition and equipment of team.	Teams consisted of 7 men and carried gun, tripod, First Aid case, 10 belt boxes (each man carrying three) two shovels and two tins of water. Each man carried on the average 4 sandbags and 2 Mills bombs. An extra supply of 4 x 2 and oil was carried with each team.
2. Ammunition supply (forward dumps, carrying parties, amount required, method of carrying).	Forward dumps were not established. From a reserve of 80 belt boxes at temporary H.Q. the runners returned from teams in the line took forward belt boxes to replace any which did not arrive at the objective. No carrying parties were required in addition to the 32 Infantry men attached for instruction. Three boxes per man were carried.
3. Water supply.	Each team carried two petrol tins of water; empty tins were sent by runner to Company H.Q. and replaced by full tins obtained from Brigade dump in exchange for empty tins.
4. Replacement of casualties and repair of guns.	Each team sent back two men on arrival at objective (after consolidation) leaving teams of 5 per gun there and men from teams in reserve were used to replace casualties. Two new guns and tripods were drawn from D.A.D.O.S. before going into action. All damaged guns were repaired by artificer where possible; if he could not repair them they were repaired by Divisional Armourer.
5. Method of advance (by bounds; on whose order; etc)	Teams advanced immediately in rear of the platoons detailed to consolidate the strong points to which guns had been allotted. Teams conformed throughout to movements of these platoons.
6. Selection of objective and sighting of gun; any direct targets?	Objectives were all detailed in Brigade Operation Orders. Guns were sighted ~~first~~ so as to obtain cross fire to cover the front in case of counter attack. Direct targets were engaged (see report from 2nd Lieut. ANDERSON attached).
7. Liaison with Infantry.	Sub section commanders worked throughout with the Commanders of the Infantry Companies with whom they advanced.

8. Communication with Company H.Q.

Each subsection had two runners who advanced with it. One afterwards returned to Company H.Q. and took all messages from there to his own subsection. The orderly with the sub section was responsible for communication back to Company H.Q.

9. Barrage Companies - Any improvements in methods to suggest?

Report on action is attached.

(sgd) M.FREEMAN, Captain,
Commanding 69th Coy.Machine Gun Corps.

3.10.17.

Instructions regarding War Diaries and Intelligence Summaries are contained in F. S. Regs., Part II. and the Staff Manual respectively. Title pages will be prepared in manuscript.

WAR DIARY
or
INTELLIGENCE SUMMARY.
(Erase heading not required.)

Army Form C. 2118.

69 M.G. Coy

Vol 21

Place	Date	Hour	Summary of Events and Information	Remarks and references to Appendices
CLAPHAM JUNCTION	2.10.17		The company was relieved in the line by 95 COY, 5th Division: the relief was conducted without loss in the middle of one of our artillery practice barrages. The company encamped for the night near RIDGEWOOD.	DA.
RIDGEWOOD	3.10.17		The company embussed at 9.30 am. and proceeded to billets in the METEREN area. The following order from G.O.C., 69th Infantry Brigade was published. "On leaving the line after the most difficult and successful fortnight this or any other Brigade has ever passed through, the Brigadier is sure that all ranks will shew on the march and at all times the same spirit of discipline and endurance that has led us to victory and will make the name of the Brigade famous in history. The Brigadier thanks all ranks for the splendid spirit they have shown throughout the long operation."	DA.
METEREN	4.10.17		Company remained in billets near METEREN.	DA
	5.10.17		" " " " " " 2/Lt J.E. MORRISON joined from the Base Depot	DA.
	6.10.17		" " " " " " During this period the company was occupied in reorganization and refitting, examination and training of reinforcements: daily parades included (a) Physical Exercises (b) Immediate Action + Mechanism (c) Judging Distance (d) Route Marches.	DA.
	7.10.17		" " " " " "	DA
	8.10.17		" " " " " "	DA
	9.10.17		" " " " " "	DA.

2353 Wt. W2544/1454 700,000 5/15 D. D. & L. A.D.S.S./Forms/C. 2118.

Army Form C. 2118.

Instructions regarding War Diaries and Intelligence Summaries are contained in F. S. Regs., Part II. and the Staff Manual respectively. Title pages will be prepared in manuscript.

WAR DIARY
or
INTELLIGENCE SUMMARY.
(Erase heading not required.)

Place	Date	Hour	Summary of Events and Information	Remarks and references to Appendices
METEREN	10.9.17		The company left billets in the METEREN area and proceeded to ONTARIO CAMP near RENINGHELST. The company left at 3.15 pm and the move was complete by 5.30 pm.	D.A.
ONTARIO CAMP	11.9.17		The company remained at ONTARIO CAMP.	DA
	12.9.17		The company left ONTARIO CAMP at 9 am and proceeded to ANZAC CAMP, 800 yards E. of CAFE BELGE arriving at 11 am. Move complete at 3 pm.	DA
	13.9.17		Company remained encamped at ANZAC CAMP.	DA
	14.9.17		" " " " " ".	DA
	15.9.17		" " " " " ". CAPT. FREEMAN M.C. and Lt. G.W. SYMES M.C. reconnoitred the line. ~~Detail~~ was made with the sandbagging of tents to afford protection against splinters from bombs and with the construction of anti aircraft emplacements.	DA
	16.9.17		The company relieved the 70th Company M.G. CORPS in the line. The company moved off from ANZAC CAMP at 5 am. to take over the POLYGON WOOD sector and the relief which was completed without loss, ~~was complete by~~ Dispositions were as follows: (a) 2/Lt H. WILSON and one subsection No 2 section had one gun at	

Instructions regarding War Diaries and Intelligence Summaries are contained in F. S. Regs., Part II. and the Staff Manual respectively. Title pages will be prepared in manuscript.

WAR DIARY
or
INTELLIGENCE SUMMARY.
(Erase heading not required.)

Army Form C. 2118.

Place	Date	Hour	Summary of Events and Information	Remarks and references to Appendices
			REF. SHEET. CHELUVELT 28 NE. 1/10,000 + WATERDAMHOEK 1/20,000	
			J 12 a 20.65 and the other at J 6 c 20.00: these guns were in the front line	
			(b). 2/Lt J.E. MORRISON in command of No. 4 section had Section HQ at J 5 d 19 95 where two guns were mounted. Other guns were at (i) JAY BARN J 5 d 10 30. (ii) J 5 c 10.60.	
			(c) 2/Lt J. TINGLE and No. 7 Section: 2 guns at J 10 b 45.55. 2 guns J 10 b 50 85.	
			(d) COY. HQ were at J 10 b 90.65.	
			Gun teams were composed of 1 N.C.O. + 5 men. Guns were taken in but tripods + belts were taken over from 70th COY. The guns under 2/Lt J TINGLE were used as barrage guns and on an S.O.S. signal being sent up opened fire on a line between J 12 d 40 20 and J 12 d 60 70.	
			The subsection in the front line was relieved every 24 hours, each day after 'STAND DOWN' in the morning	
MENIN RD.	17.10.17		Company remained in the line | During this period, shelling was very heavy in addition reliefs of the front line guns became hazardous enterprises owing to the activity of enemy snipers.	DA.
	18.10.17		" " " " "	DA.

2353 Wt. W2544/1454 700,000 5/15 D. D. & L. A.D.S.S./Forms/C. 2118.

Instructions regarding War Diaries and Intelligence Summaries are contained in F. S. Regs., Part II. and the Staff Manual respectively. Title pages will be prepared in manuscript.

WAR DIARY
or
INTELLIGENCE SUMMARY.
(Erase heading not required.)

Army Form C. 2118.

Place	Date	Hour	Summary of Events and Information	Remarks and references to Appendices
MOUND	19.10.17		Company remained in the line	D.A.
	20.10.17		" " " " "	D.A.
	21.10.17		" " " " " — The company was fortunate to suffer only 6 casualties — 2 killed and 4 wounded. During this period the remainder of the company was in ANZAC CAMP under Lt H.G. C. MEAD. The men were occupied at first in sandbagging tents, constructing AA emplacements, building latrines and incinerators and generally in preparing the camp for continuous occupation during the winter months. Latterly all available men were sent on working parties to the line.	D.A.
	22.10.17		The company was relieved in the line by 62 Coy, M.G. Corps in the early morning. The relief was conducted amidst much hostile shelling but, with the exception of 1 man wounded, the company arrived safely in ANZAC CAMP, the last man reporting by 2.30 P.M. On the same day the whole of the COMPANY transport with the exception of 3 limbered wagons, 1 A.S.C. limbered wagon + the OFFICERS' [illegible] cart set out to trek by road to WESTBECOURT in the BOISDINGHEM area.	D.A.
ANZAC CAMP	23.10.17		The company entrained at DICKIEBUSH and the remainder of the transport at VLAMERTINGHE and detrained at WIZERNES near ST OMER: they then proceeded on foot to billets in WESTBECOURT. Move complete at 6.45 p.m. Transport proceeding by road arrived at 8.30 P.M.	D.A.

2353 Wt. W2544/1454 700,000 5/15 D. D. & L. A.D.S.S./Forms/C. 2118.

Army Form C. 2118.

Instructions regarding War Diaries and Intelligence Summaries are contained in F. S. Regs., Part II. and the Staff Manual respectively. Title pages will be prepared in manuscript.

WAR DIARY
or
INTELLIGENCE SUMMARY.
(Erase heading not required.)

Place	Date	Hour	Summary of Events and Information	Remarks and references to Appendices
WESTBECOURT	24.10.17		Company remained in billets in WESTBECOURT.	D.A.
"	25.10.17		" " " " " At 10 am. the Company was inspected by G.O.C, 23rd Division. The following officer, N.C.Os and men were awarded decorations as follows :- MILITARY CROSS :- 2/Lt. D ANDERSON DISTINGUISHED CONDUCT MEDAL :- Pte M. MORGAN. MILITARY MEDAL :- Sgt. MILLS H.J. ; Cpl SHEATH W.G. ; A/Cpl GREEN H.C. ; L/Cpl ROSS T.B. ; L/Cpl MELVIN T. ; " WILSON W. ; " KENWORTHY H. ; Pte HINCHCLIFFE A	D.A.
	26.10.17		Company remained in billets in WESTBECOURT	D.A.
	27.10.17		Company remained in billets in WESTBECOURT	D.A.
	28.10.17		" " " " " "	
	29.10.17		" " " " " → On the occasion of an inspection of the 69th Infantry Brigade by G.O.C. 23rd Division, the Company paraded with the remainder of the brigade at BOISDINGHEM.	D.A.
	30.10.17		Company remained in billets at WESTBECOURT.	
	31.10.17		On this day, the Company, as part of the 69th Brigade was inspected by the COMMANDER-IN	D.A.

2353 Wt. W2544/1454 700,000 5/15 D. D. & L. A.D.S.S./Forms/C. 2118.

Army Form C. 2118.

Instructions regarding War Diaries and Intelligence Summaries are contained in F. S. Regs., Part II. and the Staff Manual respectively. Title pages will be prepared in manuscript.

WAR DIARY
or
INTELLIGENCE SUMMARY.
(Erase heading not required.)

Place	Date	Hour	Summary of Events and Information	Remarks and references to Appendices
	31.10.17		CHIEF, at LEULINGHEM. He expressed himself as agreeably surprised at, and particularly gratified with the excellent appearance made on parade by the 23rd Division after its recent exhausting experiences in the line. He considered it one of the finest divisions under his command: in sending it to ITALY, he could send no better to the help of our Allies.	
			From the 30th onwards the company was occupied in preparing for the move to ITALY. The kit of each man was completed especially in the matter of shirts, vests, pants, socks, gloves &c: all stores were made up. To harden the men up considerable route marching was done. Each section spent considerable time on the range.	D.A.
	1.11.17		Company remained in billets at WESTBECOURT. War Diary for October ends.	D.A.

[signature]
Capt.,
Commanding 69 Coy., Machine Gun Corps.

2353 Wt. W2544/1454 700,000 5/15 D. D. & L. A.D.S.S./Forms/C. 2118.

www.ingramcontent.com/pod-product-compliance
Lightning Source LLC
Chambersburg PA
CBHW081533160426
43191CB00011B/1750

9781474512701